IN TODAY'S HIGH-SPEED WORLD, MANY PEOPLE FEEL OVERSTIMULATED AND OVERWORKED, THEIR MENTAL, EMOTIONAL, AND PHYSICAL ENERGIES IN CONSTANT DEMAND. NOW, MORE THAN EVER, WE NEED TO CULTIVATE THE ABILITY TO RELAX AND RECHARGE.

There are simple actions you can take each day to dramatically improve your energy and outlook. Exercise, changes in diet, more sleep, breaks from technology, tracking accomplishments, and cultivating positive feelings for the future are just a few ways to recharge your internal batteries. By reserving time in your day for any number of these and other energy-boosting activities, you can reduce stress, increase creativity, strengthen your immune system, and keep yourself on a path of optimum health and longevity.

This 90-day journal supports your daily, intentional efforts to recharge yourself both mentally and physically. Each day is divided into two sections, "Record" and "Reflect." The first section is a place for you to record your goals, thoughts, experiences, and actions throughout your day, while the second provides an opportunity to reflect on how they contributed to your overall energy level at the end of the day. By creating a daily practice of recording and reflecting in this way, you will soon find patterns emerge that show what boosts and drains your energy. With this journal as your guide, you will learn to make meaningful changes in your daily life that will positively impact your ability to recharge and improve your quality of life.

RECORD

DATE ___ / ___ / ___

GOALS FOR TODAY:

☐ _____
☐ _____
☐ _____

TO-DOS THAT CAN WAIT:

☐ _____
☐ _____
☐ _____

I'M EXCITED ABOUT:

_____
_____
_____

I'M STRESSED ABOUT:

_____
_____
_____

HOW I SPENT MY TIME (HOURS/MINUTES):

SLEEPING: _____
ON A SCREEN: _____
EXERCISING: _____
PLAYING: _____
BEING CREATIVE: _____
RELAXING: _____

WORKING: _____
EATING: _____
FOR MYSELF: _____
WITH FAMILY: _____
SOCIALIZING: _____
OTHER: _____

FOOD/DRINK I CONSUMED TODAY:

BREAKFAST

_____
_____
_____

LUNCH

_____
_____
_____

DINNER

_____
_____
_____

WATER/CAFFEINE (GLASSES/CUPS): 1   2   3   4   5   6   7   8

REFLECT

RATE YOUR ENERGY LEVEL TODAY:

1   2   3   4   5   6   7   8   9   10

MY ENERGY LEVEL WAS HIGHEST IN THE:

MORNING   AFTERNOON   EVENING

WHAT RECHARGED ME TODAY:

- ☐ TAKING A BATH
- ☐ TAKING A NAP
- ☐ WALKING
- ☐ WORKING OUT
- ☐ STRETCHING

- ☐ JOURNALING
- ☐ SEEING A FRIEND
- ☐ TIME ALONE
- ☐ LISTENING TO MUSIC

- ☐ BEING CREATIVE
- ☐ UNPLUGGING
- ☐ TIME WITH FAMILY
- ☐ WHAT I ATE
- ☐ OTHER: _____

THIS RECHARGED ME THE MOST TODAY:

_____
_____
_____

THOUGHTS I NEED TO CLEAR TO RELAX:

_____
_____
_____

CHANGES I WANT TO MAKE FOR TOMORROW:

_____
_____
_____

RECORD

DATE ____ / ____ / ____

GOALS FOR TODAY:

☐ _____
☐ _____
☐ _____

TO-DOS THAT CAN WAIT:

☐ _____
☐ _____
☐ _____

I'M EXCITED ABOUT:

_____
_____
_____

I'M STRESSED ABOUT:

_____
_____
_____

HOW I SPENT MY TIME (HOURS/MINUTES):

SLEEPING: _____

ON A SCREEN:_____

EXERCISING:_____

PLAYING: _____

BEING CREATIVE:_____

RELAXING: _____

WORKING: _____

EATING: _____

FOR MYSELF: _____

WITH FAMILY: _____

SOCIALIZING: _____

OTHER:_____

FOOD/DRINK I CONSUMED TODAY:

BREAKFAST

_____
_____
_____

LUNCH

_____
_____
_____

DINNER

_____
_____
_____

WATER/CAFFEINE (GLASSES/CUPS): 1   2   3   4   5   6   7   8

REFLECT

RATE YOUR ENERGY LEVEL TODAY:

1   2   3   4   5   6   7   8   9   10

MY ENERGY LEVEL WAS HIGHEST IN THE:

MORNING   AFTERNOON   EVENING

WHAT RECHARGED ME TODAY:

- [ ] TAKING A BATH
- [ ] TAKING A NAP
- [ ] WALKING
- [ ] WORKING OUT
- [ ] STRETCHING

- [ ] JOURNALING
- [ ] SEEING A FRIEND
- [ ] TIME ALONE
- [ ] LISTENING TO MUSIC

- [ ] BEING CREATIVE
- [ ] UNPLUGGING
- [ ] TIME WITH FAMILY
- [ ] WHAT I ATE
- [ ] OTHER: _____

THIS RECHARGED ME THE MOST TODAY:

_____
_____
_____

THOUGHTS I NEED TO CLEAR TO RELAX:

_____
_____
_____

CHANGES I WANT TO MAKE FOR TOMORROW:

_____
_____

RECORD

DATE ___/___/___

GOALS FOR TODAY:

☐ ——————————————
☐ ——————————————
☐ ——————————————

TO-DOS THAT CAN WAIT:

☐ ——————————————
☐ ——————————————
☐ ——————————————

I'M EXCITED ABOUT:

——————————————
——————————————
——————————————

I'M STRESSED ABOUT:

——————————————
——————————————
——————————————

HOW I SPENT MY TIME (HOURS/MINUTES):

SLEEPING: _____

ON A SCREEN: _____

EXERCISING: _____

PLAYING: _____

BEING CREATIVE: _____

RELAXING: _____

WORKING: _____

EATING: _____

FOR MYSELF: _____

WITH FAMILY: _____

SOCIALIZING: _____

OTHER: _____

FOOD/DRINK I CONSUMED TODAY:

BREAKFAST

——————————
——————————
——————————

LUNCH

——————————
——————————
——————————

DINNER

——————————
——————————
——————————

WATER/CAFFEINE (GLASSES/CUPS): 1   2   3   4   5   6   7   8

REFLECT

RATE YOUR ENERGY LEVEL TODAY:

1   2   3   4   5   6   7   8   9   10

MY ENERGY LEVEL WAS HIGHEST IN THE:

MORNING   AFTERNOON   EVENING

WHAT RECHARGED ME TODAY:

- [ ] TAKING A BATH
- [ ] TAKING A NAP
- [ ] WALKING
- [ ] WORKING OUT
- [ ] STRETCHING

- [ ] JOURNALING
- [ ] SEEING A FRIEND
- [ ] TIME ALONE
- [ ] LISTENING TO MUSIC

- [ ] BEING CREATIVE
- [ ] UNPLUGGING
- [ ] TIME WITH FAMILY
- [ ] WHAT I ATE
- [ ] OTHER: _____

THIS RECHARGED ME THE MOST TODAY:

_____

_____

_____

THOUGHTS I NEED TO CLEAR TO RELAX:

_____

_____

_____

CHANGES I WANT TO MAKE FOR TOMORROW:

_____

_____

_____

RECORD

DATE ___ / ___ / ___

GOALS FOR TODAY:

- ☐ _____
- ☐ _____
- ☐ _____

TO-DOS THAT CAN WAIT:

- ☐ _____
- ☐ _____
- ☐ _____

I'M EXCITED ABOUT:

_____
_____
_____

I'M STRESSED ABOUT:

_____
_____
_____

HOW I SPENT MY TIME (HOURS/MINUTES):

SLEEPING: _____

ON A SCREEN: _____

EXERCISING: _____

PLAYING: _____

BEING CREATIVE: _____

RELAXING: _____

WORKING: _____

EATING: _____

FOR MYSELF: _____

WITH FAMILY: _____

SOCIALIZING: _____

OTHER: _____

FOOD/DRINK I CONSUMED TODAY:

BREAKFAST

_____
_____
_____

LUNCH

_____
_____
_____

DINNER

_____
_____
_____

WATER/CAFFEINE (GLASSES/CUPS):   1   2   3   4   5   6   7   8

REFLECT

RATE YOUR ENERGY LEVEL TODAY:

1   2   3   4   5   6   7   8   9   10

MY ENERGY LEVEL WAS HIGHEST IN THE:

MORNING   AFTERNOON   EVENING

WHAT RECHARGED ME TODAY:

- [ ] TAKING A BATH
- [ ] TAKING A NAP
- [ ] WALKING
- [ ] WORKING OUT
- [ ] STRETCHING

- [ ] JOURNALING
- [ ] SEEING A FRIEND
- [ ] TIME ALONE
- [ ] LISTENING TO
      MUSIC

- [ ] BEING CREATIVE
- [ ] UNPLUGGING
- [ ] TIME WITH FAMILY
- [ ] WHAT I ATE
- [ ] OTHER: _____

THIS RECHARGED ME THE MOST TODAY:

_____

_____

_____

THOUGHTS I NEED TO CLEAR TO RELAX:

_____

_____

_____

CHANGES I WANT TO MAKE FOR TOMORROW:

_____

_____

_____

RECORD

DATE ___/___/___

GOALS FOR TODAY:

☐ _____
☐ _____
☐ _____

TO-DOS THAT CAN WAIT:

☐ _____
☐ _____
☐ _____

I'M EXCITED ABOUT:

_____
_____
_____

I'M STRESSED ABOUT:

_____
_____
_____

HOW I SPENT MY TIME (HOURS/MINUTES):

SLEEPING: _____

ON A SCREEN: _____

EXERCISING: _____

PLAYING: _____

BEING CREATIVE: _____

RELAXING: _____

WORKING: _____

EATING: _____

FOR MYSELF: _____

WITH FAMILY: _____

SOCIALIZING: _____

OTHER: _____

FOOD/DRINK I CONSUMED TODAY:

BREAKFAST

_____
_____
_____

LUNCH

_____
_____
_____

DINNER

_____
_____
_____

WATER/CAFFEINE (GLASSES/CUPS): 1   2   3   4   5   6   7   8

REFLECT

RATE YOUR ENERGY LEVEL TODAY:

1   2   3   4   5   6   7   8   9   10

MY ENERGY LEVEL WAS HIGHEST IN THE:

MORNING   AFTERNOON   EVENING

WHAT RECHARGED ME TODAY:

☐ TAKING A BATH   ☐ JOURNALING   ☐ BEING CREATIVE
☐ TAKING A NAP   ☐ SEEING A FRIEND ☐ UNPLUGGING
☐ WALKING   ☐ TIME ALONE   ☐ TIME WITH FAMILY
☐ WORKING OUT   ☐ LISTENING TO   ☐ WHAT I ATE
☐ STRETCHING   MUSIC   ☐ OTHER:_____

THIS RECHARGED ME THE MOST TODAY:

_____
_____
_____

THOUGHTS I NEED TO CLEAR TO RELAX:

_____
_____
_____

CHANGES I WANT TO MAKE FOR TOMORROW:

_____
_____

RECORD

DATE ___/___/___

GOALS FOR TODAY:

☐ _____
☐ _____
☐ _____

TO-DOS THAT CAN WAIT:

☐ _____
☐ _____
☐ _____

I'M EXCITED ABOUT:

_____
_____
_____

I'M STRESSED ABOUT:

_____
_____
_____

HOW I SPENT MY TIME (HOURS/MINUTES):

SLEEPING: _____

ON A SCREEN: _____

EXERCISING: _____

PLAYING: _____

BEING CREATIVE: _____

RELAXING: _____

WORKING: _____

EATING: _____

FOR MYSELF: _____

WITH FAMILY: _____

SOCIALIZING: _____

OTHER: _____

FOOD/DRINK I CONSUMED TODAY:

BREAKFAST

_____
_____
_____

LUNCH

_____
_____
_____

DINNER

_____
_____
_____

WATER/CAFFEINE (GLASSES/CUPS): 1 2 3 4 5 6 7 8

REFLECT

RATE YOUR ENERGY LEVEL TODAY:

1   2   3   4   5   6   7   8   9   10

MY ENERGY LEVEL WAS HIGHEST IN THE:

MORNING   AFTERNOON   EVENING

WHAT RECHARGED ME TODAY:

- ☐ TAKING A BATH
- ☐ TAKING A NAP
- ☐ WALKING
- ☐ WORKING OUT
- ☐ STRETCHING

- ☐ JOURNALING
- ☐ SEEING A FRIEND
- ☐ TIME ALONE
- ☐ LISTENING TO
  MUSIC

- ☐ BEING CREATIVE
- ☐ UNPLUGGING
- ☐ TIME WITH FAMILY
- ☐ WHAT I ATE
- ☐ OTHER: _____

THIS RECHARGED ME THE MOST TODAY:

_____

_____

_____

THOUGHTS I NEED TO CLEAR TO RELAX:

_____

_____

_____

CHANGES I WANT TO MAKE FOR TOMORROW:

_____

_____

_____

RECORD

DATE ___ / ___ / ___

GOALS FOR TODAY:

- ☐ _____
- ☐ _____
- ☐ _____

TO-DOS THAT CAN WAIT:

- ☐ _____
- ☐ _____
- ☐ _____

I'M EXCITED ABOUT:

_____

_____

_____

I'M STRESSED ABOUT:

_____

_____

_____

HOW I SPENT MY TIME (HOURS/MINUTES):

SLEEPING: _____

ON A SCREEN: _____

EXERCISING: _____

PLAYING: _____

BEING CREATIVE: _____

RELAXING: _____

WORKING: _____

EATING: _____

FOR MYSELF: _____

WITH FAMILY: _____

SOCIALIZING: _____

OTHER: _____

FOOD/DRINK I CONSUMED TODAY:

BREAKFAST

_____

_____

_____

LUNCH

_____

_____

_____

DINNER

_____

_____

_____

WATER/CAFFEINE (GLASSES/CUPS): 1   2   3   4   5   6   7   8

REFLECT

RATE YOUR ENERGY LEVEL TODAY:

1   2   3   4   5   6   7   8   9   10

MY ENERGY LEVEL WAS HIGHEST IN THE:

MORNING   AFTERNOON   EVENING

WHAT RECHARGED ME TODAY:

- ☐ TAKING A BATH
- ☐ TAKING A NAP
- ☐ WALKING
- ☐ WORKING OUT
- ☐ STRETCHING

- ☐ JOURNALING
- ☐ SEEING A FRIEND
- ☐ TIME ALONE
- ☐ LISTENING TO
  MUSIC

- ☐ BEING CREATIVE
- ☐ UNPLUGGING
- ☐ TIME WITH FAMILY
- ☐ WHAT I ATE
- ☐ OTHER:_____

THIS RECHARGED ME THE MOST TODAY:

_____

_____

_____

THOUGHTS I NEED TO CLEAR TO RELAX:

_____

_____

_____

CHANGES I WANT TO MAKE FOR TOMORROW:

_____

_____

_____

RECORD

DATE ___/___/___

GOALS FOR TODAY:

☐ _____
☐ _____
☐ _____

TO-DOS THAT CAN WAIT:

☐ _____
☐ _____
☐ _____

I'M EXCITED ABOUT:

_____
_____
_____

I'M STRESSED ABOUT:

_____
_____

HOW I SPENT MY TIME (HOURS/MINUTES):

SLEEPING: _____

ON A SCREEN: _____

EXERCISING: _____

PLAYING: _____

BEING CREATIVE: _____

RELAXING: _____

WORKING: _____

EATING: _____

FOR MYSELF: _____

WITH FAMILY: _____

SOCIALIZING: _____

OTHER: _____

FOOD/DRINK I CONSUMED TODAY:

BREAKFAST

_____
_____
_____

LUNCH

_____
_____
_____

DINNER

_____
_____
_____

WATER/CAFFEINE (GLASSES/CUPS): 1   2   3   4   5   6   7   8

REFLECT

RATE YOUR ENERGY LEVEL TODAY:

1   2   3   4   5   6   7   8   9   10

MY ENERGY LEVEL WAS HIGHEST IN THE:

MORNING   AFTERNOON   EVENING

WHAT RECHARGED ME TODAY:

- [ ] TAKING A BATH
- [ ] TAKING A NAP
- [ ] WALKING
- [ ] WORKING OUT
- [ ] STRETCHING

- [ ] JOURNALING
- [ ] SEEING A FRIEND
- [ ] TIME ALONE
- [ ] LISTENING TO
       MUSIC

- [ ] BEING CREATIVE
- [ ] UNPLUGGING
- [ ] TIME WITH FAMILY
- [ ] WHAT I ATE
- [ ] OTHER: _____

THIS RECHARGED ME THE MOST TODAY:

_____

_____

_____

THOUGHTS I NEED TO CLEAR TO RELAX:

_____

_____

_____

CHANGES I WANT TO MAKE FOR TOMORROW:

_____

_____

_____

RECORD

DATE ___/___/___

GOALS FOR TODAY:

☐ _____
☐ _____
☐ _____

TO-DOS THAT CAN WAIT:

☐ _____
☐ _____
☐ _____

I'M EXCITED ABOUT:

_____
_____
_____

I'M STRESSED ABOUT:

_____
_____
_____

HOW I SPENT MY TIME (HOURS/MINUTES):

SLEEPING: _____

ON A SCREEN: _____

EXERCISING: _____

PLAYING: _____

BEING CREATIVE: _____

RELAXING: _____

WORKING: _____

EATING: _____

FOR MYSELF: _____

WITH FAMILY: _____

SOCIALIZING: _____

OTHER: _____

FOOD/DRINK I CONSUMED TODAY:

BREAKFAST

_____
_____
_____

LUNCH

_____
_____
_____

DINNER

_____
_____
_____

WATER/CAFFEINE (GLASSES/CUPS):   1   2   3   4   5   6   7   8

REFLECT

RATE YOUR ENERGY LEVEL TODAY:

1   2   3   4   5   6   7   8   9   10

MY ENERGY LEVEL WAS HIGHEST IN THE:

MORNING   AFTERNOON   EVENING

WHAT RECHARGED ME TODAY:

- [ ] TAKING A BATH
- [ ] TAKING A NAP
- [ ] WALKING
- [ ] WORKING OUT
- [ ] STRETCHING

- [ ] JOURNALING
- [ ] SEEING A FRIEND
- [ ] TIME ALONE
- [ ] LISTENING TO
  MUSIC

- [ ] BEING CREATIVE
- [ ] UNPLUGGING
- [ ] TIME WITH FAMILY
- [ ] WHAT I ATE
- [ ] OTHER: _____

THIS RECHARGED ME THE MOST TODAY:

_____

_____

_____

THOUGHTS I NEED TO CLEAR TO RELAX:

_____

_____

_____

CHANGES I WANT TO MAKE FOR TOMORROW:

_____

_____

RECORD

DATE ____ / ____ / ____

GOALS FOR TODAY:

☐ _____
☐ _____
☐ _____

TO-DOS THAT CAN WAIT:

☐ _____
☐ _____
☐ _____

I'M EXCITED ABOUT:

_____
_____
_____

I'M STRESSED ABOUT:

_____
_____
_____

HOW I SPENT MY TIME (HOURS/MINUTES):

SLEEPING: _____   WORKING: _____

ON A SCREEN: _____   EATING: _____

EXERCISING: _____   FOR MYSELF: _____

PLAYING: _____   WITH FAMILY: _____

BEING CREATIVE: _____   SOCIALIZING: _____

RELAXING: _____   OTHER: _____

FOOD/DRINK I CONSUMED TODAY:

BREAKFAST   LUNCH   DINNER

_____   _____   _____
_____   _____   _____
_____   _____   _____

WATER/CAFFEINE (GLASSES/CUPS):   1   2   3   4   5   6   7   8

REFLECT

RATE YOUR ENERGY LEVEL TODAY:

1   2   3   4   5   6   7   8   9   10

MY ENERGY LEVEL WAS HIGHEST IN THE:

MORNING   AFTERNOON   EVENING

WHAT RECHARGED ME TODAY:

☐ TAKING A BATH   ☐ JOURNALING   ☐ BEING CREATIVE
☐ TAKING A NAP   ☐ SEEING A FRIEND   ☐ UNPLUGGING
☐ WALKING   ☐ TIME ALONE   ☐ TIME WITH FAMILY
☐ WORKING OUT   ☐ LISTENING TO   ☐ WHAT I ATE
☐ STRETCHING   MUSIC   ☐ OTHER:_____

THIS RECHARGED ME THE MOST TODAY:

_____
_____
_____

THOUGHTS I NEED TO CLEAR TO RELAX:

_____
_____
_____

CHANGES I WANT TO MAKE FOR TOMORROW:

_____
_____
_____

RECORD

DATE ___ / ___ / ___

GOALS FOR TODAY:

- ☐ _____
- ☐ _____
- ☐ _____

TO-DOS THAT CAN WAIT:

- ☐ _____
- ☐ _____
- ☐ _____

I'M EXCITED ABOUT:

_____
_____
_____

I'M STRESSED ABOUT:

_____
_____
_____

HOW I SPENT MY TIME (HOURS/MINUTES):

SLEEPING: _____

ON A SCREEN: _____

EXERCISING: _____

PLAYING: _____

BEING CREATIVE: _____

RELAXING: _____

WORKING: _____

EATING: _____

FOR MYSELF: _____

WITH FAMILY: _____

SOCIALIZING: _____

OTHER: _____

FOOD/DRINK I CONSUMED TODAY:

BREAKFAST

_____
_____
_____

LUNCH

_____
_____
_____

DINNER

_____
_____
_____

WATER/CAFFEINE (GLASSES/CUPS): 1   2   3   4   5   6   7   8

REFLECT

RATE YOUR ENERGY LEVEL TODAY:

1   2   3   4   5   6   7   8   9   10

MY ENERGY LEVEL WAS HIGHEST IN THE:

MORNING   AFTERNOON   EVENING

WHAT RECHARGED ME TODAY:

☐ TAKING A BATH   ☐ JOURNALING   ☐ BEING CREATIVE
☐ TAKING A NAP   ☐ SEEING A FRIEND   ☐ UNPLUGGING
☐ WALKING   ☐ TIME ALONE   ☐ TIME WITH FAMILY
☐ WORKING OUT   ☐ LISTENING TO   ☐ WHAT I ATE
☐ STRETCHING   MUSIC   ☐ OTHER:_____

THIS RECHARGED ME THE MOST TODAY:

_____
_____
_____

THOUGHTS I NEED TO CLEAR TO RELAX:

_____
_____
_____

CHANGES I WANT TO MAKE FOR TOMORROW:

_____
_____
_____

RECORD

DATE ___/___/___

GOALS FOR TODAY:

- ☐ _____
- ☐ _____
- ☐ _____

TO-DOS THAT CAN WAIT:

- ☐ _____
- ☐ _____
- ☐ _____

I'M EXCITED ABOUT:

_____

_____

_____

I'M STRESSED ABOUT:

_____

_____

_____

HOW I SPENT MY TIME (HOURS/MINUTES):

SLEEPING:_____

ON A SCREEN:_____

EXERCISING:_____

PLAYING: _____

BEING CREATIVE:_____

RELAXING: _____

WORKING:_____

EATING: _____

FOR MYSELF: _____

WITH FAMILY: _____

SOCIALIZING: _____

OTHER:_____

FOOD/DRINK I CONSUMED TODAY:

BREAKFAST

_____

_____

_____

LUNCH

_____

_____

_____

DINNER

_____

_____

_____

WATER/CAFFEINE (GLASSES/CUPS):   1   2   3   4   5   6   7   8

REFLECT

RATE YOUR ENERGY LEVEL TODAY:

1   2   3   4   5   6   7   8   9   10

MY ENERGY LEVEL WAS HIGHEST IN THE:

MORNING   AFTERNOON   EVENING

WHAT RECHARGED ME TODAY:

- [ ] TAKING A BATH
- [ ] TAKING A NAP
- [ ] WALKING
- [ ] WORKING OUT
- [ ] STRETCHING

- [ ] JOURNALING
- [ ] SEEING A FRIEND
- [ ] TIME ALONE
- [ ] LISTENING TO
  MUSIC

- [ ] BEING CREATIVE
- [ ] UNPLUGGING
- [ ] TIME WITH FAMILY
- [ ] WHAT I ATE
- [ ] OTHER:_____

THIS RECHARGED ME THE MOST TODAY:

_____
_____
_____

THOUGHTS I NEED TO CLEAR TO RELAX:

_____
_____
_____

CHANGES I WANT TO MAKE FOR TOMORROW:

_____
_____
_____

RECORD

DATE ____ / ____ / ____

GOALS FOR TODAY:

☐ _____
☐ _____
☐ _____

TO-DOS THAT CAN WAIT:

☐ _____
☐ _____
☐ _____

I'M EXCITED ABOUT:

_____
_____
_____

I'M STRESSED ABOUT:

_____
_____
_____

HOW I SPENT MY TIME (HOURS/MINUTES):

SLEEPING: _____

ON A SCREEN: _____

EXERCISING: _____

PLAYING: _____

BEING CREATIVE: _____

RELAXING: _____

WORKING: _____

EATING: _____

FOR MYSELF: _____

WITH FAMILY: _____

SOCIALIZING: _____

OTHER: _____

FOOD/DRINK I CONSUMED TODAY:

BREAKFAST

_____
_____
_____

LUNCH

_____
_____
_____

DINNER

_____
_____
_____

WATER/CAFFEINE (GLASSES/CUPS):   1   2   3   4   5   6   7   8

REFLECT

RATE YOUR ENERGY LEVEL TODAY:

1   2   3   4   5   6   7   8   9   10

MY ENERGY LEVEL WAS HIGHEST IN THE:

MORNING   AFTERNOON   EVENING

WHAT RECHARGED ME TODAY:

- ☐ TAKING A BATH
- ☐ TAKING A NAP
- ☐ WALKING
- ☐ WORKING OUT
- ☐ STRETCHING

- ☐ JOURNALING
- ☐ SEEING A FRIEND
- ☐ TIME ALONE
- ☐ LISTENING TO
  MUSIC

- ☐ BEING CREATIVE
- ☐ UNPLUGGING
- ☐ TIME WITH FAMILY
- ☐ WHAT I ATE
- ☐ OTHER:_____

THIS RECHARGED ME THE MOST TODAY:

_____
_____
_____

THOUGHTS I NEED TO CLEAR TO RELAX:

_____
_____
_____

CHANGES I WANT TO MAKE FOR TOMORROW:

_____
_____
_____

RECORD

DATE ____/____/____

GOALS FOR TODAY:

☐ _____
☐ _____
☐ _____

TO-DOS THAT CAN WAIT:

☐ _____
☐ _____
☐ _____

I'M EXCITED ABOUT:

_____
_____
_____

I'M STRESSED ABOUT:

_____
_____
_____

HOW I SPENT MY TIME (HOURS/MINUTES):

SLEEPING: _____

ON A SCREEN: _____

EXERCISING: _____

PLAYING: _____

BEING CREATIVE: _____

RELAXING: _____

WORKING: _____

EATING: _____

FOR MYSELF: _____

WITH FAMILY: _____

SOCIALIZING: _____

OTHER: _____

FOOD/DRINK I CONSUMED TODAY:

BREAKFAST

_____
_____
_____

LUNCH

_____
_____
_____

DINNER

_____
_____
_____

WATER/CAFFEINE (GLASSES/CUPS): 1   2   3   4   5   6   7   8

REFLECT

RATE YOUR ENERGY LEVEL TODAY:

1   2   3   4   5   6   7   8   9   10

MY ENERGY LEVEL WAS HIGHEST IN THE:

MORNING   AFTERNOON   EVENING

WHAT RECHARGED ME TODAY:

- [ ] TAKING A BATH
- [ ] TAKING A NAP
- [ ] WALKING
- [ ] WORKING OUT
- [ ] STRETCHING

- [ ] JOURNALING
- [ ] SEEING A FRIEND
- [ ] TIME ALONE
- [ ] LISTENING TO MUSIC

- [ ] BEING CREATIVE
- [ ] UNPLUGGING
- [ ] TIME WITH FAMILY
- [ ] WHAT I ATE
- [ ] OTHER: _____

THIS RECHARGED ME THE MOST TODAY:

_____

_____

_____

THOUGHTS I NEED TO CLEAR TO RELAX:

_____

_____

_____

CHANGES I WANT TO MAKE FOR TOMORROW:

_____

_____

_____

RECORD

DATE ____/____/____

GOALS FOR TODAY:

- [ ] _____
- [ ] _____
- [ ] _____

TO-DOS THAT CAN WAIT:

- [ ] _____
- [ ] _____
- [ ] _____

I'M EXCITED ABOUT:

_____
_____
_____

I'M STRESSED ABOUT:

_____
_____
_____

HOW I SPENT MY TIME (HOURS/MINUTES):

SLEEPING: _____

ON A SCREEN: _____

EXERCISING: _____

PLAYING: _____

BEING CREATIVE: _____

RELAXING: _____

WORKING: _____

EATING: _____

FOR MYSELF: _____

WITH FAMILY: _____

SOCIALIZING: _____

OTHER: _____

FOOD/DRINK I CONSUMED TODAY:

BREAKFAST

_____
_____
_____

LUNCH

_____
_____
_____

DINNER

_____
_____
_____

WATER/CAFFEINE (GLASSES/CUPS): 1   2   3   4   5   6   7   8

REFLECT

RATE YOUR ENERGY LEVEL TODAY:

1   2   3   4   5   6   7   8   9   10

MY ENERGY LEVEL WAS HIGHEST IN THE:

MORNING   AFTERNOON   EVENING

WHAT RECHARGED ME TODAY:

- [ ] TAKING A BATH
- [ ] TAKING A NAP
- [ ] WALKING
- [ ] WORKING OUT
- [ ] STRETCHING

- [ ] JOURNALING
- [ ] SEEING A FRIEND
- [ ] TIME ALONE
- [ ] LISTENING TO MUSIC

- [ ] BEING CREATIVE
- [ ] UNPLUGGING
- [ ] TIME WITH FAMILY
- [ ] WHAT I ATE
- [ ] OTHER: _____

THIS RECHARGED ME THE MOST TODAY:

_____
_____
_____

THOUGHTS I NEED TO CLEAR TO RELAX:

_____
_____
_____

CHANGES I WANT TO MAKE FOR TOMORROW:

_____
_____
_____

RECORD

DATE ___ / ___ / ___

GOALS FOR TODAY:

☐ _____
☐ _____
☐ _____

TO-DOS THAT CAN WAIT:

☐ _____
☐ _____
☐ _____

I'M EXCITED ABOUT:

_____
_____
_____

I'M STRESSED ABOUT:

_____
_____
_____

HOW I SPENT MY TIME (HOURS/MINUTES):

SLEEPING: _____

ON A SCREEN: _____

EXERCISING: _____

PLAYING: _____

BEING CREATIVE: _____

RELAXING: _____

WORKING: _____

EATING: _____

FOR MYSELF: _____

WITH FAMILY: _____

SOCIALIZING: _____

OTHER: _____

FOOD/DRINK I CONSUMED TODAY:

BREAKFAST

_____
_____
_____

LUNCH

_____
_____
_____

DINNER

_____
_____
_____

WATER/CAFFEINE (GLASSES/CUPS):   1   2   3   4   5   6   7   8

REFLECT

RATE YOUR ENERGY LEVEL TODAY:

1   2   3   4   5   6   7   8   9   10

MY ENERGY LEVEL WAS HIGHEST IN THE:

MORNING   AFTERNOON   EVENING

WHAT RECHARGED ME TODAY:

☐ TAKING A BATH   ☐ JOURNALING   ☐ BEING CREATIVE
☐ TAKING A NAP   ☐ SEEING A FRIEND   ☐ UNPLUGGING
☐ WALKING   ☐ TIME ALONE   ☐ TIME WITH FAMILY
☐ WORKING OUT   ☐ LISTENING TO   ☐ WHAT I ATE
☐ STRETCHING   MUSIC   ☐ OTHER:_____

THIS RECHARGED ME THE MOST TODAY:
_____
_____
_____

THOUGHTS I NEED TO CLEAR TO RELAX:
_____
_____
_____

CHANGES I WANT TO MAKE FOR TOMORROW:
_____
_____
_____

RECORD

DATE ___ / ___ /___

GOALS FOR TODAY:

- ☐ ——————————————
- ☐ ——————————————
- ☐ ——————————————

TO-DOS THAT CAN WAIT:

- ☐ ——————————————
- ☐ ——————————————
- ☐ ——————————————

I'M EXCITED ABOUT:

————————————————
————————————————
————————————————

I'M STRESSED ABOUT:

————————————————
————————————————
————————————————

HOW I SPENT MY TIME (HOURS/MINUTES):

SLEEPING: _____

ON A SCREEN: _____

EXERCISING: _____

PLAYING: _____

BEING CREATIVE: _____

RELAXING: _____

WORKING: _____

EATING: _____

FOR MYSELF: _____

WITH FAMILY: _____

SOCIALIZING: _____

OTHER: _____

FOOD/DRINK I CONSUMED TODAY:

BREAKFAST

————————————
————————————
————————————

LUNCH

————————————
————————————
————————————

DINNER

————————————
————————————
————————————

WATER/CAFFEINE (GLASSES/CUPS):   1   2   3   4   5   6   7   8

REFLECT

RATE YOUR ENERGY LEVEL TODAY:

1   2   3   4   5   6   7   8   9   10

MY ENERGY LEVEL WAS HIGHEST IN THE:

MORNING   AFTERNOON   EVENING

WHAT RECHARGED ME TODAY:

- ☐ TAKING A BATH
- ☐ TAKING A NAP
- ☐ WALKING
- ☐ WORKING OUT
- ☐ STRETCHING

- ☐ JOURNALING
- ☐ SEEING A FRIEND
- ☐ TIME ALONE
- ☐ LISTENING TO
  MUSIC

- ☐ BEING CREATIVE
- ☐ UNPLUGGING
- ☐ TIME WITH FAMILY
- ☐ WHAT I ATE
- ☐ OTHER:_____

THIS RECHARGED ME THE MOST TODAY:

_____

_____

_____

THOUGHTS I NEED TO CLEAR TO RELAX:

_____

_____

_____

CHANGES I WANT TO MAKE FOR TOMORROW:

_____

_____

_____

RECORD

DATE ___/___/___

GOALS FOR TODAY:

☐ _____
☐ _____
☐ _____

TO-DOS THAT CAN WAIT:

☐ _____
☐ _____
☐ _____

I'M EXCITED ABOUT:

_____
_____
_____

I'M STRESSED ABOUT:

_____
_____
_____

HOW I SPENT MY TIME (HOURS/MINUTES):

SLEEPING: _____

ON A SCREEN: _____

EXERCISING: _____

PLAYING: _____

BEING CREATIVE: _____

RELAXING: _____

WORKING: _____

EATING: _____

FOR MYSELF: _____

WITH FAMILY: _____

SOCIALIZING: _____

OTHER: _____

FOOD/DRINK I CONSUMED TODAY:

BREAKFAST

_____
_____
_____

LUNCH

_____
_____
_____

DINNER

_____
_____
_____

WATER/CAFFEINE (GLASSES/CUPS): 1   2   3   4   5   6   7   8

REFLECT

RATE YOUR ENERGY LEVEL TODAY:

1   2   3   4   5   6   7   8   9   10

MY ENERGY LEVEL WAS HIGHEST IN THE:

MORNING   AFTERNOON   EVENING

WHAT RECHARGED ME TODAY:

- ☐ TAKING A BATH
- ☐ TAKING A NAP
- ☐ WALKING
- ☐ WORKING OUT
- ☐ STRETCHING

- ☐ JOURNALING
- ☐ SEEING A FRIEND
- ☐ TIME ALONE
- ☐ LISTENING TO MUSIC

- ☐ BEING CREATIVE
- ☐ UNPLUGGING
- ☐ TIME WITH FAMILY
- ☐ WHAT I ATE
- ☐ OTHER: _____

THIS RECHARGED ME THE MOST TODAY:

_____

_____

_____

THOUGHTS I NEED TO CLEAR TO RELAX:

_____

_____

_____

CHANGES I WANT TO MAKE FOR TOMORROW:

_____

_____

_____

RECORD

DATE ___/___/___

GOALS FOR TODAY:

☐ _____
☐ _____
☐ _____

TO-DOS THAT CAN WAIT:

☐ _____
☐ _____
☐ _____

I'M EXCITED ABOUT:

_____
_____
_____

I'M STRESSED ABOUT:

_____
_____
_____

HOW I SPENT MY TIME (HOURS/MINUTES):

SLEEPING: _____

ON A SCREEN: _____

EXERCISING: _____

PLAYING: _____

BEING CREATIVE: _____

RELAXING: _____

WORKING: _____

EATING: _____

FOR MYSELF: _____

WITH FAMILY: _____

SOCIALIZING: _____

OTHER: _____

FOOD/DRINK I CONSUMED TODAY:

BREAKFAST

_____
_____
_____

LUNCH

_____
_____
_____

DINNER

_____
_____
_____

WATER/CAFFEINE (GLASSES/CUPS):   1   2   3   4   5   6   7   8

REFLECT

MY ENERGY LEVEL WAS HIGHEST IN THE:
MORNING   AFTERNOON   EVENING

WHAT RECHARGED ME TODAY:

- ☐ TAKING A BATH
- ☐ TAKING A NAP
- ☐ WALKING
- ☐ WORKING OUT
- ☐ STRETCHING

- ☐ JOURNALING
- ☐ SEEING A FRIEND
- ☐ TIME ALONE
- ☐ LISTENING TO MUSIC

- ☐ BEING CREATIVE
- ☐ UNPLUGGING
- ☐ TIME WITH FAMILY
- ☐ WHAT I ATE
- ☐ OTHER:_____

THIS RECHARGED ME THE MOST TODAY:
_____
_____
_____

THOUGHTS I NEED TO CLEAR TO RELAX:
_____
_____
_____

CHANGES I WANT TO MAKE FOR TOMORROW:
_____
_____
_____

RECORD

DATE ____/____/____

GOALS FOR TODAY:

- ☐ _____
- ☐ _____
- ☐ _____

TO-DOS THAT CAN WAIT:

- ☐ _____
- ☐ _____
- ☐ _____

I'M EXCITED ABOUT:

_____
_____
_____

I'M STRESSED ABOUT:

_____
_____
_____

HOW I SPENT MY TIME (HOURS/MINUTES):

SLEEPING: _____

ON A SCREEN: _____

EXERCISING: _____

PLAYING: _____

BEING CREATIVE: _____

RELAXING: _____

WORKING: _____

EATING: _____

FOR MYSELF: _____

WITH FAMILY: _____

SOCIALIZING: _____

OTHER: _____

FOOD/DRINK I CONSUMED TODAY:

BREAKFAST

_____
_____
_____

LUNCH

_____
_____
_____

DINNER

_____
_____
_____

WATER/CAFFEINE (GLASSES/CUPS): 1   2   3   4   5   6   7   8

REFLECT

RATE YOUR ENERGY LEVEL TODAY:

1   2   3   4   5   6   7   8   9   10

MY ENERGY LEVEL WAS HIGHEST IN THE:

MORNING   AFTERNOON   EVENING

WHAT RECHARGED ME TODAY:

- ☐ TAKING A BATH
- ☐ TAKING A NAP
- ☐ WALKING
- ☐ WORKING OUT
- ☐ STRETCHING

- ☐ JOURNALING
- ☐ SEEING A FRIEND
- ☐ TIME ALONE
- ☐ LISTENING TO MUSIC

- ☐ BEING CREATIVE
- ☐ UNPLUGGING
- ☐ TIME WITH FAMILY
- ☐ WHAT I ATE
- ☐ OTHER:_____

THIS RECHARGED ME THE MOST TODAY:

_____
_____
_____

THOUGHTS I NEED TO CLEAR TO RELAX:

_____
_____
_____

CHANGES I WANT TO MAKE FOR TOMORROW:

_____
_____
_____

RECORD

GOALS FOR TODAY:

☐ _____
☐ _____
☐ _____

TO-DOS THAT CAN WAIT:

☐ _____
☐ _____
☐ _____

I'M EXCITED ABOUT:

_____
_____
_____

I'M STRESSED ABOUT:

_____
_____
_____

HOW I SPENT MY TIME (HOURS/MINUTES):

SLEEPING: _____

ON A SCREEN: _____

EXERCISING: _____

PLAYING: _____

BEING CREATIVE: _____

RELAXING: _____

WORKING: _____

EATING: _____

FOR MYSELF: _____

WITH FAMILY: _____

SOCIALIZING: _____

OTHER: _____

FOOD/DRINK I CONSUMED TODAY:

BREAKFAST

_____
_____
_____

LUNCH

_____
_____
_____

DINNER

_____
_____
_____

WATER/CAFFEINE (GLASSES/CUPS): 1   2   3   4   5   6   7   8

REFLECT

RATE YOUR ENERGY LEVEL TODAY:

1   2   3   4   5   6   7   8   9   10

MY ENERGY LEVEL WAS HIGHEST IN THE:

MORNING   AFTERNOON   EVENING

WHAT RECHARGED ME TODAY:

☐ TAKING A BATH   ☐ JOURNALING   ☐ BEING CREATIVE
☐ TAKING A NAP   ☐ SEEING A FRIEND   ☐ UNPLUGGING
☐ WALKING   ☐ TIME ALONE   ☐ TIME WITH FAMILY
☐ WORKING OUT   ☐ LISTENING TO   ☐ WHAT I ATE
☐ STRETCHING   MUSIC   ☐ OTHER: _____

THIS RECHARGED ME THE MOST TODAY:

_____
_____
_____

THOUGHTS I NEED TO CLEAR TO RELAX:

_____
_____
_____

CHANGES I WANT TO MAKE FOR TOMORROW:

_____
_____

RECORD

DATE ___/___/___

GOALS FOR TODAY:

- ☐ _____
- ☐ _____
- ☐ _____

TO-DOS THAT CAN WAIT:

- ☐ _____
- ☐ _____
- ☐ _____

I'M EXCITED ABOUT:

_____

_____

_____

I'M STRESSED ABOUT:

_____

_____

_____

HOW I SPENT MY TIME (HOURS/MINUTES):

SLEEPING: _____

ON A SCREEN: _____

EXERCISING: _____

PLAYING: _____

BEING CREATIVE: _____

RELAXING: _____

WORKING: _____

EATING: _____

FOR MYSELF: _____

WITH FAMILY: _____

SOCIALIZING: _____

OTHER: _____

FOOD/DRINK I CONSUMED TODAY:

BREAKFAST

_____

_____

_____

LUNCH

_____

_____

_____

DINNER

_____

_____

_____

WATER/CAFFEINE (GLASSES/CUPS): 1 2 3 4 5 6 7 8

REFLECT

MY ENERGY LEVEL WAS HIGHEST IN THE:

MORNING   AFTERNOON   EVENING

WHAT RECHARGED ME TODAY:

- [ ] TAKING A BATH
- [ ] TAKING A NAP
- [ ] WALKING
- [ ] WORKING OUT
- [ ] STRETCHING

- [ ] JOURNALING
- [ ] SEEING A FRIEND
- [ ] TIME ALONE
- [ ] LISTENING TO MUSIC

- [ ] BEING CREATIVE
- [ ] UNPLUGGING
- [ ] TIME WITH FAMILY
- [ ] WHAT I ATE
- [ ] OTHER: _____

THIS RECHARGED ME THE MOST TODAY:

_____
_____
_____

THOUGHTS I NEED TO CLEAR TO RELAX:

_____
_____
_____

CHANGES I WANT TO MAKE FOR TOMORROW:

_____
_____
_____

RECORD

DATE ___/___/___

GOALS FOR TODAY:

☐ _____
☐ _____
☐ _____

TO-DOS THAT CAN WAIT:

☐ _____
☐ _____
☐ _____

I'M EXCITED ABOUT:

_____
_____
_____

I'M STRESSED ABOUT:

_____
_____
_____

HOW I SPENT MY TIME (HOURS/MINUTES):

SLEEPING: _____   WORKING: _____
ON A SCREEN: _____   EATING: _____
EXERCISING: _____   FOR MYSELF: _____
PLAYING: _____   WITH FAMILY: _____
BEING CREATIVE: _____   SOCIALIZING: _____
RELAXING: _____   OTHER: _____

FOOD/DRINK I CONSUMED TODAY:

BREAKFAST   LUNCH   DINNER

_____   _____   _____
_____   _____   _____
_____   _____   _____

WATER/CAFFEINE (GLASSES/CUPS):   1   2   3   4   5   6   7   8

REFLECT

RATE YOUR ENERGY LEVEL TODAY:

1   2   3   4   5   6   7   8   9   10

MY ENERGY LEVEL WAS HIGHEST IN THE:

MORNING   AFTERNOON   EVENING

WHAT RECHARGED ME TODAY:

- [ ] TAKING A BATH
- [ ] TAKING A NAP
- [ ] WALKING
- [ ] WORKING OUT
- [ ] STRETCHING

- [ ] JOURNALING
- [ ] SEEING A FRIEND
- [ ] TIME ALONE
- [ ] LISTENING TO MUSIC

- [ ] BEING CREATIVE
- [ ] UNPLUGGING
- [ ] TIME WITH FAMILY
- [ ] WHAT I ATE
- [ ] OTHER: _____

THIS RECHARGED ME THE MOST TODAY:

_____
_____
_____

THOUGHTS I NEED TO CLEAR TO RELAX:

_____
_____
_____

CHANGES I WANT TO MAKE FOR TOMORROW:

_____
_____
_____

RECORD

GOALS FOR TODAY:

☐ _____
☐ _____
☐ _____

TO-DOS THAT CAN WAIT:

☐ _____
☐ _____
☐ _____

I'M EXCITED ABOUT:

_____
_____
_____

I'M STRESSED ABOUT:

_____
_____
_____

HOW I SPENT MY TIME (HOURS/MINUTES):

SLEEPING: _____
ON A SCREEN: _____
EXERCISING: _____
PLAYING: _____
BEING CREATIVE: _____
RELAXING: _____

WORKING: _____
EATING: _____
FOR MYSELF: _____
WITH FAMILY: _____
SOCIALIZING: _____
OTHER: _____

FOOD/DRINK I CONSUMED TODAY:

BREAKFAST

_____
_____
_____

LUNCH

_____
_____
_____

DINNER

_____
_____
_____

WATER/CAFFEINE (GLASSES/CUPS): 1   2   3   4   5   6   7   8

REFLECT

RATE YOUR ENERGY LEVEL TODAY:

1   2   3   4   5   6   7   8   9   10

MY ENERGY LEVEL WAS HIGHEST IN THE:

MORNING   AFTERNOON   EVENING

WHAT RECHARGED ME TODAY:

☐ TAKING A BATH   ☐ JOURNALING   ☐ BEING CREATIVE
☐ TAKING A NAP   ☐ SEEING A FRIEND   ☐ UNPLUGGING
☐ WALKING   ☐ TIME ALONE   ☐ TIME WITH FAMILY
☐ WORKING OUT   ☐ LISTENING TO   ☐ WHAT I ATE
☐ STRETCHING   MUSIC   ☐ OTHER:_____

THIS RECHARGED ME THE MOST TODAY:

_____
_____
_____

THOUGHTS I NEED TO CLEAR TO RELAX:

_____
_____
_____

CHANGES I WANT TO MAKE FOR TOMORROW:

_____
_____
_____

RECORD

DATE ___ / ___ / ___

GOALS FOR TODAY:

- ☐ ————————————
- ☐ ————————————
- ☐ ————————————

TO-DOS THAT CAN WAIT:

- ☐ ————————————
- ☐ ————————————
- ☐ ————————————

I'M EXCITED ABOUT:

————————————————
————————————————
————————————————

I'M STRESSED ABOUT:

————————————————
————————————————
————————————————

HOW I SPENT MY TIME (HOURS/MINUTES):

SLEEPING: _____

ON A SCREEN: _____

EXERCISING: _____

PLAYING: _____

BEING CREATIVE: _____

RELAXING: _____

WORKING: _____

EATING: _____

FOR MYSELF: _____

WITH FAMILY: _____

SOCIALIZING: _____

OTHER: _____

FOOD/DRINK I CONSUMED TODAY:

BREAKFAST

————————————
————————————
————————————

LUNCH

————————————
————————————
————————————

DINNER

————————————
————————————
————————————

WATER/CAFFEINE (GLASSES/CUPS):   1   2   3   4   5   6   7   8

REFLECT

RATE YOUR ENERGY LEVEL TODAY:

1   2   3   4   5   6   7   8   9   10

MY ENERGY LEVEL WAS HIGHEST IN THE:

MORNING   AFTERNOON   EVENING

WHAT RECHARGED ME TODAY:

☐ TAKING A BATH   ☐ JOURNALING   ☐ BEING CREATIVE
☐ TAKING A NAP   ☐ SEEING A FRIEND ☐ UNPLUGGING
☐ WALKING   ☐ TIME ALONE   ☐ TIME WITH FAMILY
☐ WORKING OUT   ☐ LISTENING TO   ☐ WHAT I ATE
☐ STRETCHING   MUSIC   ☐ OTHER:_____

THIS RECHARGED ME THE MOST TODAY:

_____
_____
_____

THOUGHTS I NEED TO CLEAR TO RELAX:

_____
_____
_____

CHANGES I WANT TO MAKE FOR TOMORROW:

_____
_____
_____

RECORD

DATE ___ / ___ / ___

GOALS FOR TODAY:

☐ _____
☐ _____
☐ _____

TO-DOS THAT CAN WAIT:

☐ _____
☐ _____
☐ _____

I'M EXCITED ABOUT:

_____
_____
_____

I'M STRESSED ABOUT:

_____
_____
_____

HOW I SPENT MY TIME (HOURS/MINUTES):

SLEEPING: _____

ON A SCREEN: _____

EXERCISING: _____

PLAYING: _____

BEING CREATIVE: _____

RELAXING: _____

WORKING: _____

EATING: _____

FOR MYSELF: _____

WITH FAMILY: _____

SOCIALIZING: _____

OTHER: _____

FOOD/DRINK I CONSUMED TODAY:

BREAKFAST

_____
_____
_____

LUNCH

_____
_____
_____

DINNER

_____
_____
_____

WATER/CAFFEINE (GLASSES/CUPS): 1   2   3   4   5   6   7   8

REFLECT

RATE YOUR ENERGY LEVEL TODAY:

1   2   3   4   5   6   7   8   9   10

MY ENERGY LEVEL WAS HIGHEST IN THE:

MORNING   AFTERNOON   EVENING

WHAT RECHARGED ME TODAY:

☐ TAKING A BATH   ☐ JOURNALING   ☐ BEING CREATIVE
☐ TAKING A NAP   ☐ SEEING A FRIEND   ☐ UNPLUGGING
☐ WALKING   ☐ TIME ALONE   ☐ TIME WITH FAMILY
☐ WORKING OUT   ☐ LISTENING TO   ☐ WHAT I ATE
☐ STRETCHING   MUSIC   ☐ OTHER:_____

THIS RECHARGED ME THE MOST TODAY:

_____
_____
_____

THOUGHTS I NEED TO CLEAR TO RELAX:

_____
_____
_____

CHANGES I WANT TO MAKE FOR TOMORROW:

_____
_____
_____

RECORD

DATE ___/___/___

GOALS FOR TODAY:

☐ _____
☐ _____
☐ _____

TO-DOS THAT CAN WAIT:

☐ _____
☐ _____
☐ _____

I'M EXCITED ABOUT:

_____
_____
_____

I'M STRESSED ABOUT:

_____
_____
_____

HOW I SPENT MY TIME (HOURS/MINUTES):

SLEEPING: _____

ON A SCREEN: _____

EXERCISING: _____

PLAYING: _____

BEING CREATIVE: _____

RELAXING: _____

WORKING: _____

EATING: _____

FOR MYSELF: _____

WITH FAMILY: _____

SOCIALIZING: _____

OTHER: _____

FOOD/DRINK I CONSUMED TODAY:

BREAKFAST

_____
_____
_____

LUNCH

_____
_____
_____

DINNER

_____
_____
_____

WATER/CAFFEINE (GLASSES/CUPS): 1   2   3   4   5   6   7   8

REFLECT

RATE YOUR ENERGY LEVEL TODAY:

1   2   3   4   5   6   7   8   9   10

MY ENERGY LEVEL WAS HIGHEST IN THE:

MORNING   AFTERNOON   EVENING

WHAT RECHARGED ME TODAY:

☐ TAKING A BATH   ☐ JOURNALING   ☐ BEING CREATIVE
☐ TAKING A NAP   ☐ SEEING A FRIEND   ☐ UNPLUGGING
☐ WALKING   ☐ TIME ALONE   ☐ TIME WITH FAMILY
☐ WORKING OUT   ☐ LISTENING TO   ☐ WHAT I ATE
☐ STRETCHING   MUSIC   ☐ OTHER:_____

THIS RECHARGED ME THE MOST TODAY:
_____
_____
_____

THOUGHTS I NEED TO CLEAR TO RELAX:
_____
_____
_____

CHANGES I WANT TO MAKE FOR TOMORROW:
_____
_____
_____

RECORD

GOALS FOR TODAY:

☐ _____
☐ _____
☐ _____

TO-DOS THAT CAN WAIT:

☐ _____
☐ _____
☐ _____

I'M EXCITED ABOUT:

_____
_____
_____

I'M STRESSED ABOUT:

_____
_____
_____

HOW I SPENT MY TIME (HOURS/MINUTES):

SLEEPING: _____

ON A SCREEN: _____

EXERCISING: _____

PLAYING: _____

BEING CREATIVE: _____

RELAXING: _____

WORKING: _____

EATING: _____

FOR MYSELF: _____

WITH FAMILY: _____

SOCIALIZING: _____

OTHER: _____

FOOD/DRINK I CONSUMED TODAY:

BREAKFAST

_____
_____
_____

LUNCH

_____
_____
_____

DINNER

_____
_____
_____

WATER/CAFFEINE (GLASSES/CUPS): 1   2   3   4   5   6   7   8

REFLECT

RATE YOUR ENERGY LEVEL TODAY:

1   2   3   4   5   6   7   8   9   10

MY ENERGY LEVEL WAS HIGHEST IN THE:

MORNING   AFTERNOON   EVENING

WHAT RECHARGED ME TODAY:

- ☐ TAKING A BATH
- ☐ TAKING A NAP
- ☐ WALKING
- ☐ WORKING OUT
- ☐ STRETCHING

- ☐ JOURNALING
- ☐ SEEING A FRIEND
- ☐ TIME ALONE
- ☐ LISTENING TO MUSIC

- ☐ BEING CREATIVE
- ☐ UNPLUGGING
- ☐ TIME WITH FAMILY
- ☐ WHAT I ATE
- ☐ OTHER:_____

THIS RECHARGED ME THE MOST TODAY:
_____
_____
_____

THOUGHTS I NEED TO CLEAR TO RELAX:
_____
_____
_____

CHANGES I WANT TO MAKE FOR TOMORROW:
_____
_____
_____

RECORD

DATE ___/___/___

GOALS FOR TODAY:

☐ ——————————————
☐ ——————————————
☐ ——————————————

TO-DOS THAT CAN WAIT:

☐ ——————————————
☐ ——————————————
☐ ——————————————

I'M EXCITED ABOUT:

————————————————
————————————————
————————————————

I'M STRESSED ABOUT:

————————————————
————————————————
————————————————

HOW I SPENT MY TIME (HOURS/MINUTES):

SLEEPING: _____

ON A SCREEN: _____

EXERCISING: _____

PLAYING: _____

BEING CREATIVE: _____

RELAXING: _____

WORKING: _____

EATING: _____

FOR MYSELF: _____

WITH FAMILY: _____

SOCIALIZING: _____

OTHER: _____

FOOD/DRINK I CONSUMED TODAY:

BREAKFAST

————————————
————————————
————————————

LUNCH

————————————
————————————
————————————

DINNER

————————————
————————————
————————————

WATER/CAFFEINE (GLASSES/CUPS): 1 2 3 4 5 6 7 8

REFLECT

RATE YOUR ENERGY LEVEL TODAY:

1   2   3   4   5   6   7   8   9   10

MY ENERGY LEVEL WAS HIGHEST IN THE:

MORNING   AFTERNOON   EVENING

WHAT RECHARGED ME TODAY:

☐ TAKING A BATH   ☐ JOURNALING   ☐ BEING CREATIVE
☐ TAKING A NAP   ☐ SEEING A FRIEND ☐ UNPLUGGING
☐ WALKING   ☐ TIME ALONE   ☐ TIME WITH FAMILY
☐ WORKING OUT   ☐ LISTENING TO   ☐ WHAT I ATE
☐ STRETCHING   MUSIC   ☐ OTHER:_____

THIS RECHARGED ME THE MOST TODAY:

_____
_____
_____

THOUGHTS I NEED TO CLEAR TO RELAX:

_____
_____
_____

CHANGES I WANT TO MAKE FOR TOMORROW:

_____
_____
_____

RECORD

DATE ___ / ___ / ___

GOALS FOR TODAY:

☐ _____
☐ _____
☐ _____

TO-DOS THAT CAN WAIT:

☐ _____
☐ _____
☐ _____

I'M EXCITED ABOUT:

_____
_____
_____

I'M STRESSED ABOUT:

_____
_____
_____

HOW I SPENT MY TIME (HOURS/MINUTES):

SLEEPING: _____

ON A SCREEN: _____

EXERCISING: _____

PLAYING: _____

BEING CREATIVE: _____

RELAXING: _____

WORKING: _____

EATING: _____

FOR MYSELF: _____

WITH FAMILY: _____

SOCIALIZING: _____

OTHER: _____

FOOD/DRINK I CONSUMED TODAY:

BREAKFAST

_____
_____
_____

LUNCH

_____
_____
_____

DINNER

_____
_____
_____

WATER/CAFFEINE (GLASSES/CUPS): 1 2 3 4 5 6 7 8

REFLECT

RATE YOUR ENERGY LEVEL TODAY:

1   2   3   4   5   6   7   8   9   10

MY ENERGY LEVEL WAS HIGHEST IN THE:

MORNING   AFTERNOON   EVENING

WHAT RECHARGED ME TODAY:

☐ TAKING A BATH   ☐ JOURNALING   ☐ BEING CREATIVE
☐ TAKING A NAP   ☐ SEEING A FRIEND   ☐ UNPLUGGING
☐ WALKING   ☐ TIME ALONE   ☐ TIME WITH FAMILY
☐ WORKING OUT   ☐ LISTENING TO   ☐ WHAT I ATE
☐ STRETCHING   MUSIC   ☐ OTHER:_____

THIS RECHARGED ME THE MOST TODAY:

_____
_____
_____

THOUGHTS I NEED TO CLEAR TO RELAX:

_____
_____
_____

CHANGES I WANT TO MAKE FOR TOMORROW:

_____
_____
_____

RECORD

DATE ___ / ___ / ___

GOALS FOR TODAY:

☐ _____
☐ _____
☐ _____

TO-DOS THAT CAN WAIT:

☐ _____
☐ _____
☐ _____

I'M EXCITED ABOUT:

_____
_____
_____

I'M STRESSED ABOUT:

_____
_____
_____

HOW I SPENT MY TIME (HOURS/MINUTES):

SLEEPING: _____
ON A SCREEN: _____
EXERCISING: _____
PLAYING: _____
BEING CREATIVE: _____
RELAXING: _____

WORKING: _____
EATING: _____
FOR MYSELF: _____
WITH FAMILY: _____
SOCIALIZING: _____
OTHER: _____

FOOD/DRINK I CONSUMED TODAY:

BREAKFAST

_____
_____
_____

LUNCH

_____
_____
_____

DINNER

_____
_____
_____

WATER/CAFFEINE (GLASSES/CUPS):   1   2   3   4   5   6   7   8

REFLECT

RATE YOUR ENERGY LEVEL TODAY:

1   2   3   4   5   6   7   8   9   10

MY ENERGY LEVEL WAS HIGHEST IN THE:

MORNING   AFTERNOON   EVENING

WHAT RECHARGED ME TODAY:

- ☐ TAKING A BATH
- ☐ TAKING A NAP
- ☐ WALKING
- ☐ WORKING OUT
- ☐ STRETCHING

- ☐ JOURNALING
- ☐ SEEING A FRIEND
- ☐ TIME ALONE
- ☐ LISTENING TO MUSIC

- ☐ BEING CREATIVE
- ☐ UNPLUGGING
- ☐ TIME WITH FAMILY
- ☐ WHAT I ATE
- ☐ OTHER: _____

THIS RECHARGED ME THE MOST TODAY:

_____

_____

_____

THOUGHTS I NEED TO CLEAR TO RELAX:

_____

_____

_____

CHANGES I WANT TO MAKE FOR TOMORROW:

_____

_____

_____

RECORD

DATE ___/___/___

GOALS FOR TODAY:

☐ _____
☐ _____
☐ _____

TO-DOS THAT CAN WAIT:

☐ _____
☐ _____
☐ _____

I'M EXCITED ABOUT:

_____
_____
_____

I'M STRESSED ABOUT:

_____
_____
_____

HOW I SPENT MY TIME (HOURS/MINUTES):

SLEEPING: _____

ON A SCREEN: _____

EXERCISING: _____

PLAYING: _____

BEING CREATIVE: _____

RELAXING: _____

WORKING: _____

EATING: _____

FOR MYSELF: _____

WITH FAMILY: _____

SOCIALIZING: _____

OTHER: _____

FOOD/DRINK I CONSUMED TODAY:

BREAKFAST

_____
_____
_____

LUNCH

_____
_____
_____

DINNER

_____
_____
_____

WATER/CAFFEINE (GLASSES/CUPS): 1   2   3   4   5   6   7   8

REFLECT

RATE YOUR ENERGY LEVEL TODAY:

1   2   3   4   5   6   7   8   9   10

MY ENERGY LEVEL WAS HIGHEST IN THE:

MORNING   AFTERNOON   EVENING

WHAT RECHARGED ME TODAY:

☐ TAKING A BATH   ☐ JOURNALING   ☐ BEING CREATIVE
☐ TAKING A NAP   ☐ SEEING A FRIEND ☐ UNPLUGGING
☐ WALKING   ☐ TIME ALONE   ☐ TIME WITH FAMILY
☐ WORKING OUT   ☐ LISTENING TO   ☐ WHAT I ATE
☐ STRETCHING   MUSIC   ☐ OTHER:_____

THIS RECHARGED ME THE MOST TODAY:

_____
_____
_____

THOUGHTS I NEED TO CLEAR TO RELAX:

_____
_____
_____

CHANGES I WANT TO MAKE FOR TOMORROW:

_____
_____
_____

RECORD

DATE ____/____/____

GOALS FOR TODAY:

☐ _____
☐ _____
☐ _____

TO-DOS THAT CAN WAIT:

☐ _____
☐ _____
☐ _____

I'M EXCITED ABOUT:

_____
_____
_____

I'M STRESSED ABOUT:

_____
_____
_____

HOW I SPENT MY TIME (HOURS/MINUTES):

SLEEPING: _____   WORKING: _____

ON A SCREEN: _____   EATING: _____

EXERCISING: _____   FOR MYSELF: _____

PLAYING: _____   WITH FAMILY: _____

BEING CREATIVE: _____ SOCIALIZING: _____

RELAXING: _____   OTHER: _____

FOOD/DRINK I CONSUMED TODAY:

BREAKFAST   LUNCH   DINNER

_____   _____   _____
_____   _____   _____
_____   _____   _____

WATER/CAFFEINE (GLASSES/CUPS):   1   2   3   4   5   6   7   8

REFLECT

RATE YOUR ENERGY LEVEL TODAY:

1   2   3   4   5   6   7   8   9   10

MY ENERGY LEVEL WAS HIGHEST IN THE:

MORNING   AFTERNOON   EVENING

WHAT RECHARGED ME TODAY:

☐ TAKING A BATH   ☐ JOURNALING   ☐ BEING CREATIVE
☐ TAKING A NAP   ☐ SEEING A FRIEND   ☐ UNPLUGGING
☐ WALKING   ☐ TIME ALONE   ☐ TIME WITH FAMILY
☐ WORKING OUT   ☐ LISTENING TO   ☐ WHAT I ATE
☐ STRETCHING   MUSIC   ☐ OTHER: _____

THIS RECHARGED ME THE MOST TODAY:

_____
_____
_____

THOUGHTS I NEED TO CLEAR TO RELAX:

_____
_____
_____

CHANGES I WANT TO MAKE FOR TOMORROW:

_____
_____
_____

RECORD

DATE ___/___/___

GOALS FOR TODAY:

☐ ————————————————
☐ ————————————————
☐ ————————————————

TO-DOS THAT CAN WAIT:

☐ ————————————————
☐ ————————————————
☐ ————————————————

I'M EXCITED ABOUT:

————————————————————
————————————————————
————————————————————

I'M STRESSED ABOUT:

————————————————————
————————————————————
————————————————————

HOW I SPENT MY TIME (HOURS/MINUTES):

SLEEPING: _____

ON A SCREEN: _____

EXERCISING: _____

PLAYING: _____

BEING CREATIVE: _____

RELAXING: _____

WORKING: _____

EATING: _____

FOR MYSELF: _____

WITH FAMILY: _____

SOCIALIZING: _____

OTHER: _____

FOOD/DRINK I CONSUMED TODAY:

BREAKFAST

————————————————
————————————————
————————————————

LUNCH

————————————————
————————————————
————————————————

DINNER

————————————————
————————————————
————————————————

WATER/CAFFEINE (GLASSES/CUPS): 1   2   3   4   5   6   7   8

REFLECT

RATE YOUR ENERGY LEVEL TODAY:

1   2   3   4   5   6   7   8   9   10

MY ENERGY LEVEL WAS HIGHEST IN THE:

MORNING   AFTERNOON   EVENING

WHAT RECHARGED ME TODAY:

☐ TAKING A BATH   ☐ JOURNALING   ☐ BEING CREATIVE
☐ TAKING A NAP   ☐ SEEING A FRIEND   ☐ UNPLUGGING
☐ WALKING   ☐ TIME ALONE   ☐ TIME WITH FAMILY
☐ WORKING OUT   ☐ LISTENING TO   ☐ WHAT I ATE
☐ STRETCHING   MUSIC   ☐ OTHER: _____

THIS RECHARGED ME THE MOST TODAY:

_____
_____
_____

THOUGHTS I NEED TO CLEAR TO RELAX:

_____
_____
_____

CHANGES I WANT TO MAKE FOR TOMORROW:

_____
_____
_____

RECORD

DATE ____ / ____ / ____

GOALS FOR TODAY:

☐ _____
☐ _____
☐ _____

TO-DOS THAT CAN WAIT:

☐ _____
☐ _____
☐ _____

I'M EXCITED ABOUT:

_____
_____
_____

I'M STRESSED ABOUT:

_____
_____
_____

HOW I SPENT MY TIME (HOURS/MINUTES):

SLEEPING: _____

ON A SCREEN: _____

EXERCISING: _____

PLAYING: _____

BEING CREATIVE: _____

RELAXING: _____

WORKING: _____

EATING: _____

FOR MYSELF: _____

WITH FAMILY: _____

SOCIALIZING: _____

OTHER: _____

FOOD/DRINK I CONSUMED TODAY:

BREAKFAST

_____
_____
_____

LUNCH

_____
_____
_____

DINNER

_____
_____
_____

WATER/CAFFEINE (GLASSES/CUPS): 1 2 3 4 5 6 7 8

REFLECT

RATE YOUR ENERGY LEVEL TODAY:

1   2   3   4   5   6   7   8   9   10

MY ENERGY LEVEL WAS HIGHEST IN THE:

MORNING   AFTERNOON   EVENING

WHAT RECHARGED ME TODAY:

- [ ] TAKING A BATH
- [ ] TAKING A NAP
- [ ] WALKING
- [ ] WORKING OUT
- [ ] STRETCHING

- [ ] JOURNALING
- [ ] SEEING A FRIEND
- [ ] TIME ALONE
- [ ] LISTENING TO
      MUSIC

- [ ] BEING CREATIVE
- [ ] UNPLUGGING
- [ ] TIME WITH FAMILY
- [ ] WHAT I ATE
- [ ] OTHER: _____

THIS RECHARGED ME THE MOST TODAY:

_____

_____

_____

THOUGHTS I NEED TO CLEAR TO RELAX:

_____

_____

_____

CHANGES I WANT TO MAKE FOR TOMORROW:

_____

_____

_____

RECORD

DATE ___ / ___ / ___

GOALS FOR TODAY:

☐ _____
☐ _____
☐ _____

TO-DOS THAT CAN WAIT:

☐ _____
☐ _____
☐ _____

I'M EXCITED ABOUT:

_____
_____
_____

I'M STRESSED ABOUT:

_____
_____
_____

HOW I SPENT MY TIME (HOURS/MINUTES):

SLEEPING: _____   WORKING: _____

ON A SCREEN: _____   EATING: _____

EXERCISING: _____   FOR MYSELF: _____

PLAYING: _____   WITH FAMILY: _____

BEING CREATIVE: _____   SOCIALIZING: _____

RELAXING: _____   OTHER: _____

FOOD/DRINK I CONSUMED TODAY:

BREAKFAST   LUNCH   DINNER

_____   _____   _____
_____   _____   _____
_____   _____   _____

WATER/CAFFEINE (GLASSES/CUPS): 1 2 3 4 5 6 7 8

REFLECT

RATE YOUR ENERGY LEVEL TODAY:

1   2   3   4   5   6   7   8   9   10

MY ENERGY LEVEL WAS HIGHEST IN THE:

MORNING   AFTERNOON   EVENING

WHAT RECHARGED ME TODAY:

- ☐ TAKING A BATH
- ☐ TAKING A NAP
- ☐ WALKING
- ☐ WORKING OUT
- ☐ STRETCHING

- ☐ JOURNALING
- ☐ SEEING A FRIEND
- ☐ TIME ALONE
- ☐ LISTENING TO
   MUSIC

- ☐ BEING CREATIVE
- ☐ UNPLUGGING
- ☐ TIME WITH FAMILY
- ☐ WHAT I ATE
- ☐ OTHER: _____

THIS RECHARGED ME THE MOST TODAY:

_____

_____

_____

THOUGHTS I NEED TO CLEAR TO RELAX:

_____

_____

_____

CHANGES I WANT TO MAKE FOR TOMORROW:

_____

_____

_____

RECORD

DATE ___/___/___

GOALS FOR TODAY:

☐ _____
☐ _____
☐ _____

TO-DOS THAT CAN WAIT:

☐ _____
☐ _____
☐ _____

I'M EXCITED ABOUT:

_____
_____
_____

I'M STRESSED ABOUT:

_____
_____
_____

HOW I SPENT MY TIME (HOURS/MINUTES):

SLEEPING:_____

ON A SCREEN:_____

EXERCISING:_____

PLAYING: _____

BEING CREATIVE:_____

RELAXING: _____

WORKING:_____

EATING: _____

FOR MYSELF: _____

WITH FAMILY: _____

SOCIALIZING: _____

OTHER:_____

FOOD/DRINK I CONSUMED TODAY:

BREAKFAST

_____
_____
_____

LUNCH

_____
_____
_____

DINNER

_____
_____
_____

WATER/CAFFEINE (GLASSES/CUPS): 1 2 3 4 5 6 7 8

REFLECT

RATE YOUR ENERGY LEVEL TODAY:

1   2   3   4   5   6   7   8   9   10

MY ENERGY LEVEL WAS HIGHEST IN THE:

MORNING   AFTERNOON   EVENING

WHAT RECHARGED ME TODAY:

☐ TAKING A BATH   ☐ JOURNALING   ☐ BEING CREATIVE
☐ TAKING A NAP   ☐ SEEING A FRIEND   ☐ UNPLUGGING
☐ WALKING   ☐ TIME ALONE   ☐ TIME WITH FAMILY
☐ WORKING OUT   ☐ LISTENING TO   ☐ WHAT I ATE
☐ STRETCHING   MUSIC   ☐ OTHER:_____

THIS RECHARGED ME THE MOST TODAY:

_____

_____

_____

THOUGHTS I NEED TO CLEAR TO RELAX:

_____

_____

_____

CHANGES I WANT TO MAKE FOR TOMORROW:

_____

_____

_____

RECORD

GOALS FOR TODAY:

☐ _____
☐ _____
☐ _____

TO-DOS THAT CAN WAIT:

☐ _____
☐ _____
☐ _____

I'M EXCITED ABOUT:

_____
_____
_____

I'M STRESSED ABOUT:

_____
_____
_____

HOW I SPENT MY TIME (HOURS/MINUTES):

SLEEPING: _____

ON A SCREEN: _____

EXERCISING: _____

PLAYING: _____

BEING CREATIVE: _____

RELAXING: _____

WORKING: _____

EATING: _____

FOR MYSELF: _____

WITH FAMILY: _____

SOCIALIZING: _____

OTHER: _____

FOOD/DRINK I CONSUMED TODAY:

BREAKFAST

_____
_____
_____

LUNCH

_____
_____
_____

DINNER

_____
_____
_____

WATER/CAFFEINE (GLASSES/CUPS): 1   2   3   4   5   6   7   8

REFLECT

RATE YOUR ENERGY LEVEL TODAY:

1   2   3   4   5   6   7   8   9   10

MY ENERGY LEVEL WAS HIGHEST IN THE:

MORNING   AFTERNOON   EVENING

WHAT RECHARGED ME TODAY:

- [ ] TAKING A BATH
- [ ] TAKING A NAP
- [ ] WALKING
- [ ] WORKING OUT
- [ ] STRETCHING

- [ ] JOURNALING
- [ ] SEEING A FRIEND
- [ ] TIME ALONE
- [ ] LISTENING TO MUSIC

- [ ] BEING CREATIVE
- [ ] UNPLUGGING
- [ ] TIME WITH FAMILY
- [ ] WHAT I ATE
- [ ] OTHER: _____

THIS RECHARGED ME THE MOST TODAY:

_____

_____

_____

THOUGHTS I NEED TO CLEAR TO RELAX:

_____

_____

_____

CHANGES I WANT TO MAKE FOR TOMORROW:

_____

_____

_____

RECORD

DATE ___/___/___

GOALS FOR TODAY:

☐ _____
☐ _____
☐ _____

TO-DOS THAT CAN WAIT:

☐ _____
☐ _____
☐ _____

I'M EXCITED ABOUT:

_____
_____
_____

I'M STRESSED ABOUT:

_____
_____
_____

HOW I SPENT MY TIME (HOURS/MINUTES):

SLEEPING: _____

ON A SCREEN: _____

EXERCISING: _____

PLAYING: _____

BEING CREATIVE: _____

RELAXING: _____

WORKING: _____

EATING: _____

FOR MYSELF: _____

WITH FAMILY: _____

SOCIALIZING: _____

OTHER: _____

FOOD/DRINK I CONSUMED TODAY:

BREAKFAST

_____
_____
_____

LUNCH

_____
_____
_____

DINNER

_____
_____
_____

WATER/CAFFEINE (GLASSES/CUPS): 1 2 3 4 5 6 7 8

REFLECT

RATE YOUR ENERGY LEVEL TODAY:

1   2   3   4   5   6   7   8   9   10

MY ENERGY LEVEL WAS HIGHEST IN THE:

MORNING   AFTERNOON   EVENING

WHAT RECHARGED ME TODAY:

☐ TAKING A BATH   ☐ JOURNALING   ☐ BEING CREATIVE
☐ TAKING A NAP   ☐ SEEING A FRIEND   ☐ UNPLUGGING
☐ WALKING   ☐ TIME ALONE   ☐ TIME WITH FAMILY
☐ WORKING OUT   ☐ LISTENING TO   ☐ WHAT I ATE
☐ STRETCHING   MUSIC   ☐ OTHER: _____

THIS RECHARGED ME THE MOST TODAY:

_____
_____
_____

THOUGHTS I NEED TO CLEAR TO RELAX:

_____
_____
_____

CHANGES I WANT TO MAKE FOR TOMORROW:

_____
_____
_____

RECORD

DATE ___/___/___

GOALS FOR TODAY:

☐ _____
☐ _____
☐ _____

TO-DOS THAT CAN WAIT:

☐ _____
☐ _____
☐ _____

I'M EXCITED ABOUT:

_____
_____
_____

I'M STRESSED ABOUT:

_____
_____
_____

HOW I SPENT MY TIME (HOURS/MINUTES):

SLEEPING: _____

ON A SCREEN: _____

EXERCISING: _____

PLAYING: _____

BEING CREATIVE: _____

RELAXING: _____

WORKING: _____

EATING: _____

FOR MYSELF: _____

WITH FAMILY: _____

SOCIALIZING: _____

OTHER: _____

FOOD/DRINK I CONSUMED TODAY:

BREAKFAST

_____
_____
_____

LUNCH

_____
_____
_____

DINNER

_____
_____
_____

WATER/CAFFEINE (GLASSES/CUPS): 1   2   3   4   5   6   7   8

REFLECT

RATE YOUR ENERGY LEVEL TODAY:

1   2   3   4   5   6   7   8   9   10

MY ENERGY LEVEL WAS HIGHEST IN THE:

MORNING   AFTERNOON   EVENING

WHAT RECHARGED ME TODAY:

- ☐ TAKING A BATH
- ☐ TAKING A NAP
- ☐ WALKING
- ☐ WORKING OUT
- ☐ STRETCHING

- ☐ JOURNALING
- ☐ SEEING A FRIEND
- ☐ TIME ALONE
- ☐ LISTENING TO
   MUSIC

- ☐ BEING CREATIVE
- ☐ UNPLUGGING
- ☐ TIME WITH FAMILY
- ☐ WHAT I ATE
- ☐ OTHER:_____

THIS RECHARGED ME THE MOST TODAY:

_____

_____

_____

THOUGHTS I NEED TO CLEAR TO RELAX:

_____

_____

_____

CHANGES I WANT TO MAKE FOR TOMORROW:

_____

_____

_____

RECORD

DATE ___/___/___

GOALS FOR TODAY:

☐ _____
☐ _____
☐ _____

TO-DOS THAT CAN WAIT:

☐ _____
☐ _____
☐ _____

I'M EXCITED ABOUT:

_____
_____
_____

I'M STRESSED ABOUT:

_____
_____
_____

HOW I SPENT MY TIME (HOURS/MINUTES):

SLEEPING: _____ WORKING: _____

ON A SCREEN: _____ EATING: _____

EXERCISING: _____ FOR MYSELF: _____

PLAYING: _____ WITH FAMILY: _____

BEING CREATIVE: _____ SOCIALIZING: _____

RELAXING: _____ OTHER: _____

FOOD/DRINK I CONSUMED TODAY:

BREAKFAST

_____
_____
_____

LUNCH

_____
_____
_____

DINNER

_____
_____
_____

WATER/CAFFEINE (GLASSES/CUPS): 1 2 3 4 5 6 7 8

REFLECT

RATE YOUR ENERGY LEVEL TODAY:

1   2   3   4   5   6   7   8   9   10

MY ENERGY LEVEL WAS HIGHEST IN THE:

MORNING   AFTERNOON   EVENING

WHAT RECHARGED ME TODAY:

- ☐ TAKING A BATH
- ☐ TAKING A NAP
- ☐ WALKING
- ☐ WORKING OUT
- ☐ STRETCHING
- ☐ JOURNALING
- ☐ SEEING A FRIEND
- ☐ TIME ALONE
- ☐ LISTENING TO MUSIC
- ☐ BEING CREATIVE
- ☐ UNPLUGGING
- ☐ TIME WITH FAMILY
- ☐ WHAT I ATE
- ☐ OTHER: _____

THIS RECHARGED ME THE MOST TODAY:

_____

_____

_____

THOUGHTS I NEED TO CLEAR TO RELAX:

_____

_____

_____

CHANGES I WANT TO MAKE FOR TOMORROW:

_____

_____

_____

RECORD

DATE ___ / ___ / ___

GOALS FOR TODAY:

- ☐ _____
- ☐ _____
- ☐ _____

TO-DOS THAT CAN WAIT:

- ☐ _____
- ☐ _____
- ☐ _____

I'M EXCITED ABOUT:

_____
_____
_____

I'M STRESSED ABOUT:

_____
_____
_____

HOW I SPENT MY TIME (HOURS/MINUTES):

SLEEPING: _____

ON A SCREEN: _____

EXERCISING: _____

PLAYING: _____

BEING CREATIVE: _____

RELAXING: _____

WORKING: _____

EATING: _____

FOR MYSELF: _____

WITH FAMILY: _____

SOCIALIZING: _____

OTHER: _____

FOOD/DRINK I CONSUMED TODAY:

BREAKFAST

_____
_____
_____

LUNCH

_____
_____
_____

DINNER

_____
_____
_____

WATER/CAFFEINE (GLASSES/CUPS): 1   2   3   4   5   6   7   8

REFLECT

RATE YOUR ENERGY LEVEL TODAY:

1   2   3   4   5   6   7   8   9   10

MY ENERGY LEVEL WAS HIGHEST IN THE:

MORNING   AFTERNOON   EVENING

WHAT RECHARGED ME TODAY:

☐ TAKING A BATH   ☐ JOURNALING   ☐ BEING CREATIVE
☐ TAKING A NAP   ☐ SEEING A FRIEND   ☐ UNPLUGGING
☐ WALKING   ☐ TIME ALONE   ☐ TIME WITH FAMILY
☐ WORKING OUT   ☐ LISTENING TO   ☐ WHAT I ATE
☐ STRETCHING   MUSIC   ☐ OTHER:_____

THIS RECHARGED ME THE MOST TODAY:

_____
_____
_____

THOUGHTS I NEED TO CLEAR TO RELAX:

_____
_____
_____

CHANGES I WANT TO MAKE FOR TOMORROW:

_____
_____
_____

RECORD

DATE ___/___/___

GOALS FOR TODAY:

- ☐ _____
- ☐ _____
- ☐ _____

TO-DOS THAT CAN WAIT:

- ☐ _____
- ☐ _____
- ☐ _____

I'M EXCITED ABOUT:

_____

_____

_____

I'M STRESSED ABOUT:

_____

_____

_____

HOW I SPENT MY TIME (HOURS/MINUTES):

SLEEPING: _____

ON A SCREEN: _____

EXERCISING: _____

PLAYING: _____

BEING CREATIVE: _____

RELAXING: _____

WORKING: _____

EATING: _____

FOR MYSELF: _____

WITH FAMILY: _____

SOCIALIZING: _____

OTHER: _____

FOOD/DRINK I CONSUMED TODAY:

BREAKFAST

_____

_____

_____

LUNCH

_____

_____

_____

DINNER

_____

_____

_____

WATER/CAFFEINE (GLASSES/CUPS): 1   2   3   4   5   6   7   8

REFLECT

RATE YOUR ENERGY LEVEL TODAY:

1   2   3   4   5   6   7   8   9   10

MY ENERGY LEVEL WAS HIGHEST IN THE:

MORNING   AFTERNOON   EVENING

WHAT RECHARGED ME TODAY:

☐ TAKING A BATH   ☐ JOURNALING   ☐ BEING CREATIVE
☐ TAKING A NAP   ☐ SEEING A FRIEND   ☐ UNPLUGGING
☐ WALKING   ☐ TIME ALONE   ☐ TIME WITH FAMILY
☐ WORKING OUT   ☐ LISTENING TO   ☐ WHAT I ATE
☐ STRETCHING   MUSIC   ☐ OTHER: _____

THIS RECHARGED ME THE MOST TODAY:

_____
_____
_____

THOUGHTS I NEED TO CLEAR TO RELAX:

_____
_____
_____

CHANGES I WANT TO MAKE FOR TOMORROW:

_____
_____
_____

RECORD

DATE ___ / ___ / ___

GOALS FOR TODAY:

☐ ——————————————
☐ ——————————————
☐ ——————————————

TO-DOS THAT CAN WAIT:

☐ ——————————————
☐ ——————————————
☐ ——————————————

I'M EXCITED ABOUT:

——————————————
——————————————
——————————————

I'M STRESSED ABOUT:

——————————————
——————————————
——————————————

HOW I SPENT MY TIME (HOURS/MINUTES):

SLEEPING: _____

ON A SCREEN: _____

EXERCISING: _____

PLAYING: _____

BEING CREATIVE: _____

RELAXING: _____

WORKING: _____

EATING: _____

FOR MYSELF: _____

WITH FAMILY: _____

SOCIALIZING: _____

OTHER: _____

FOOD/DRINK I CONSUMED TODAY:

BREAKFAST

——————————
——————————
——————————

LUNCH

——————————
——————————
——————————

DINNER

——————————
——————————
——————————

WATER/CAFFEINE (GLASSES/CUPS): 1 2 3 4 5 6 7 8

REFLECT

RATE YOUR ENERGY LEVEL TODAY:

1   2   3   4   5   6   7   8   9   10

MY ENERGY LEVEL WAS HIGHEST IN THE:

MORNING   AFTERNOON   EVENING

WHAT RECHARGED ME TODAY:

☐ TAKING A BATH   ☐ JOURNALING   ☐ BEING CREATIVE
☐ TAKING A NAP   ☐ SEEING A FRIEND   ☐ UNPLUGGING
☐ WALKING   ☐ TIME ALONE   ☐ TIME WITH FAMILY
☐ WORKING OUT   ☐ LISTENING TO   ☐ WHAT I ATE
☐ STRETCHING   MUSIC   ☐ OTHER:_____

THIS RECHARGED ME THE MOST TODAY:
_____
_____
_____

THOUGHTS I NEED TO CLEAR TO RELAX:
_____
_____
_____

CHANGES I WANT TO MAKE FOR TOMORROW:
_____
_____
_____

RECORD

DATE ___/___/___

GOALS FOR TODAY:

☐ _____
☐ _____
☐ _____

TO-DOS THAT CAN WAIT:

☐ _____
☐ _____
☐ _____

I'M EXCITED ABOUT:

_____
_____
_____

I'M STRESSED ABOUT:

_____
_____
_____

HOW I SPENT MY TIME (HOURS/MINUTES):

SLEEPING: _____

ON A SCREEN: _____

EXERCISING: _____

PLAYING: _____

BEING CREATIVE: _____

RELAXING: _____

WORKING: _____

EATING: _____

FOR MYSELF: _____

WITH FAMILY: _____

SOCIALIZING: _____

OTHER: _____

FOOD/DRINK I CONSUMED TODAY:

BREAKFAST

_____
_____
_____

LUNCH

_____
_____
_____

DINNER

_____
_____
_____

WATER/CAFFEINE (GLASSES/CUPS): 1 2 3 4 5 6 7 8

REFLECT

RATE YOUR ENERGY LEVEL TODAY:

1   2   3   4   5   6   7   8   9   10

MY ENERGY LEVEL WAS HIGHEST IN THE:

MORNING   AFTERNOON   EVENING

WHAT RECHARGED ME TODAY:

☐ TAKING A BATH   ☐ JOURNALING   ☐ BEING CREATIVE
☐ TAKING A NAP   ☐ SEEING A FRIEND ☐ UNPLUGGING
☐ WALKING   ☐ TIME ALONE   ☐ TIME WITH FAMILY
☐ WORKING OUT   ☐ LISTENING TO   ☐ WHAT I ATE
☐ STRETCHING   MUSIC   ☐ OTHER:_____

THIS RECHARGED ME THE MOST TODAY:

_____
_____
_____

THOUGHTS I NEED TO CLEAR TO RELAX:

_____
_____
_____

CHANGES I WANT TO MAKE FOR TOMORROW:

_____
_____
_____

RECORD

DATE ___/___/___

GOALS FOR TODAY:

☐ _____
☐ _____
☐ _____

TO-DOS THAT CAN WAIT:

☐ _____
☐ _____
☐ _____

I'M EXCITED ABOUT:

_____
_____
_____

I'M STRESSED ABOUT:

_____
_____
_____

HOW I SPENT MY TIME (HOURS/MINUTES):

SLEEPING: _____   WORKING: _____

ON A SCREEN: _____   EATING: _____

EXERCISING: _____   FOR MYSELF: _____

PLAYING: _____   WITH FAMILY: _____

BEING CREATIVE: _____   SOCIALIZING: _____

RELAXING: _____   OTHER: _____

FOOD/DRINK I CONSUMED TODAY:

BREAKFAST   LUNCH   DINNER

_____   _____   _____
_____   _____   _____
_____   _____   _____

WATER/CAFFEINE (GLASSES/CUPS):   1   2   3   4   5   6   7   8

REFLECT

RATE YOUR ENERGY LEVEL TODAY:

1   2   3   4   5   6   7   8   9   10

MY ENERGY LEVEL WAS HIGHEST IN THE:

MORNING   AFTERNOON   EVENING

WHAT RECHARGED ME TODAY:

☐ TAKING A BATH   ☐ JOURNALING   ☐ BEING CREATIVE
☐ TAKING A NAP   ☐ SEEING A FRIEND ☐ UNPLUGGING
☐ WALKING   ☐ TIME ALONE   ☐ TIME WITH FAMILY
☐ WORKING OUT   ☐ LISTENING TO   ☐ WHAT I ATE
☐ STRETCHING   MUSIC   ☐ OTHER:_____

THIS RECHARGED ME THE MOST TODAY:

_____
_____
_____

THOUGHTS I NEED TO CLEAR TO RELAX:

_____
_____
_____

CHANGES I WANT TO MAKE FOR TOMORROW:

_____
_____
_____

RECORD

DATE ___/___/___

GOALS FOR TODAY:

☐ _____
☐ _____
☐ _____

TO-DOS THAT CAN WAIT:

☐ _____
☐ _____
☐ _____

I'M EXCITED ABOUT:

_____
_____
_____

I'M STRESSED ABOUT:

_____
_____
_____

HOW I SPENT MY TIME (HOURS/MINUTES):

SLEEPING: _____

ON A SCREEN: _____

EXERCISING: _____

PLAYING: _____

BEING CREATIVE: _____

RELAXING: _____

WORKING: _____

EATING: _____

FOR MYSELF: _____

WITH FAMILY: _____

SOCIALIZING: _____

OTHER: _____

FOOD/DRINK I CONSUMED TODAY:

BREAKFAST

_____
_____
_____

LUNCH

_____
_____
_____

DINNER

_____
_____
_____

WATER/CAFFEINE (GLASSES/CUPS):   1   2   3   4   5   6   7   8

REFLECT

RATE YOUR ENERGY LEVEL TODAY:

1   2   3   4   5   6   7   8   9   10

MY ENERGY LEVEL WAS HIGHEST IN THE:

MORNING   AFTERNOON   EVENING

WHAT RECHARGED ME TODAY:

- ☐ TAKING A BATH
- ☐ TAKING A NAP
- ☐ WALKING
- ☐ WORKING OUT
- ☐ STRETCHING

- ☐ JOURNALING
- ☐ SEEING A FRIEND
- ☐ TIME ALONE
- ☐ LISTENING TO
  MUSIC

- ☐ BEING CREATIVE
- ☐ UNPLUGGING
- ☐ TIME WITH FAMILY
- ☐ WHAT I ATE
- ☐ OTHER: _____

THIS RECHARGED ME THE MOST TODAY:

_____

_____

_____

THOUGHTS I NEED TO CLEAR TO RELAX:

_____

_____

_____

CHANGES I WANT TO MAKE FOR TOMORROW:

_____

_____

_____

RECORD

DATE ___/___/___

GOALS FOR TODAY:

☐ _____
☐ _____
☐ _____

TO-DOS THAT CAN WAIT:

☐ _____
☐ _____
☐ _____

I'M EXCITED ABOUT:

_____
_____
_____

I'M STRESSED ABOUT:

_____
_____
_____

HOW I SPENT MY TIME (HOURS/MINUTES):

SLEEPING: _____
ON A SCREEN: _____
EXERCISING: _____
PLAYING: _____
BEING CREATIVE: _____
RELAXING: _____

WORKING: _____
EATING: _____
FOR MYSELF: _____
WITH FAMILY: _____
SOCIALIZING: _____
OTHER: _____

FOOD/DRINK I CONSUMED TODAY:

BREAKFAST

_____
_____
_____

LUNCH

_____
_____
_____

DINNER

_____
_____
_____

WATER/CAFFEINE (GLASSES/CUPS): 1   2   3   4   5   6   7   8

REFLECT

RATE YOUR ENERGY LEVEL TODAY:

1   2   3   4   5   6   7   8   9   10

MY ENERGY LEVEL WAS HIGHEST IN THE:

MORNING   AFTERNOON   EVENING

WHAT RECHARGED ME TODAY:

☐ TAKING A BATH   ☐ JOURNALING   ☐ BEING CREATIVE
☐ TAKING A NAP   ☐ SEEING A FRIEND   ☐ UNPLUGGING
☐ WALKING   ☐ TIME ALONE   ☐ TIME WITH FAMILY
☐ WORKING OUT   ☐ LISTENING TO   ☐ WHAT I ATE
☐ STRETCHING   MUSIC   ☐ OTHER:_____

THIS RECHARGED ME THE MOST TODAY:
_____
_____
_____

THOUGHTS I NEED TO CLEAR TO RELAX:
_____
_____
_____

CHANGES I WANT TO MAKE FOR TOMORROW:
_____
_____
_____

RECORD

GOALS FOR TODAY:

☐ _____
☐ _____
☐ _____

TO-DOS THAT CAN WAIT:

☐ _____
☐ _____
☐ _____

I'M EXCITED ABOUT:

_____
_____
_____

I'M STRESSED ABOUT:

_____
_____
_____

HOW I SPENT MY TIME (HOURS/MINUTES):

SLEEPING: _____

ON A SCREEN: _____

EXERCISING: _____

PLAYING: _____

BEING CREATIVE: _____

RELAXING: _____

WORKING: _____

EATING: _____

FOR MYSELF: _____

WITH FAMILY: _____

SOCIALIZING: _____

OTHER: _____

FOOD/DRINK I CONSUMED TODAY:

BREAKFAST

_____
_____
_____

LUNCH

_____
_____
_____

DINNER

_____
_____
_____

WATER/CAFFEINE (GLASSES/CUPS):   1   2   3   4   5   6   7   8

REFLECT

RATE YOUR ENERGY LEVEL TODAY:

1   2   3   4   5   6   7   8   9   10

MY ENERGY LEVEL WAS HIGHEST IN THE:

MORNING   AFTERNOON   EVENING

WHAT RECHARGED ME TODAY:

☐ TAKING A BATH   ☐ JOURNALING   ☐ BEING CREATIVE
☐ TAKING A NAP   ☐ SEEING A FRIEND ☐ UNPLUGGING
☐ WALKING   ☐ TIME ALONE   ☐ TIME WITH FAMILY
☐ WORKING OUT   ☐ LISTENING TO   ☐ WHAT I ATE
☐ STRETCHING   MUSIC   ☐ OTHER:_____

THIS RECHARGED ME THE MOST TODAY:

_____
_____
_____

THOUGHTS I NEED TO CLEAR TO RELAX:

_____
_____
_____

CHANGES I WANT TO MAKE FOR TOMORROW:

_____
_____
_____

RECORD

DATE ___ / ___ / ___

GOALS FOR TODAY:

☐ _____
☐ _____
☐ _____

TO-DOS THAT CAN WAIT:

☐ _____
☐ _____
☐ _____

I'M EXCITED ABOUT:

_____
_____
_____

I'M STRESSED ABOUT:

_____
_____
_____

HOW I SPENT MY TIME (HOURS/MINUTES):

SLEEPING: _____

ON A SCREEN: _____

EXERCISING: _____

PLAYING: _____

BEING CREATIVE: _____

RELAXING: _____

WORKING: _____

EATING: _____

FOR MYSELF: _____

WITH FAMILY: _____

SOCIALIZING: _____

OTHER: _____

FOOD/DRINK I CONSUMED TODAY:

BREAKFAST

_____
_____
_____

LUNCH

_____
_____
_____

DINNER

_____
_____
_____

WATER/CAFFEINE (GLASSES/CUPS): 1   2   3   4   5   6   7   8

REFLECT

RATE YOUR ENERGY LEVEL TODAY:

1   2   3   4   5   6   7   8   9   10

MY ENERGY LEVEL WAS HIGHEST IN THE:

MORNING   AFTERNOON   EVENING

WHAT RECHARGED ME TODAY:

- [ ] TAKING A BATH
- [ ] TAKING A NAP
- [ ] WALKING
- [ ] WORKING OUT
- [ ] STRETCHING

- [ ] JOURNALING
- [ ] SEEING A FRIEND
- [ ] TIME ALONE
- [ ] LISTENING TO
      MUSIC

- [ ] BEING CREATIVE
- [ ] UNPLUGGING
- [ ] TIME WITH FAMILY
- [ ] WHAT I ATE
- [ ] OTHER:_____

THIS RECHARGED ME THE MOST TODAY:

_____
_____
_____

THOUGHTS I NEED TO CLEAR TO RELAX:

_____
_____
_____

CHANGES I WANT TO MAKE FOR TOMORROW:

_____
_____
_____

RECORD

DATE ___ / ___ / ___

GOALS FOR TODAY:

☐ ————————————————
☐ ————————————————
☐ ————————————————

TO-DOS THAT CAN WAIT:

☐ ————————————————
☐ ————————————————
☐ ————————————————

I'M EXCITED ABOUT:

————————————————
————————————————
————————————————

I'M STRESSED ABOUT:

————————————————
————————————————
————————————————

HOW I SPENT MY TIME (HOURS/MINUTES):

SLEEPING:_____

ON A SCREEN:_____

EXERCISING:_____

PLAYING: _____

BEING CREATIVE:_____

RELAXING: _____

WORKING:_____

EATING: _____

FOR MYSELF: _____

WITH FAMILY: _____

SOCIALIZING: _____

OTHER:_____

FOOD/DRINK I CONSUMED TODAY:

BREAKFAST

————————————
————————————
————————————

LUNCH

————————————
————————————
————————————

DINNER

————————————
————————————
————————————

WATER/CAFFEINE (GLASSES/CUPS):   1   2   3   4   5   6   7   8

REFLECT

RATE YOUR ENERGY LEVEL TODAY:

1   2   3   4   5   6   7   8   9   10

MY ENERGY LEVEL WAS HIGHEST IN THE:

MORNING   AFTERNOON   EVENING

WHAT RECHARGED ME TODAY:

- ☐ TAKING A BATH
- ☐ TAKING A NAP
- ☐ WALKING
- ☐ WORKING OUT
- ☐ STRETCHING

- ☐ JOURNALING
- ☐ SEEING A FRIEND
- ☐ TIME ALONE
- ☐ LISTENING TO
    MUSIC

- ☐ BEING CREATIVE
- ☐ UNPLUGGING
- ☐ TIME WITH FAMILY
- ☐ WHAT I ATE
- ☐ OTHER: _____

THIS RECHARGED ME THE MOST TODAY:

_____

_____

_____

THOUGHTS I NEED TO CLEAR TO RELAX:

_____

_____

_____

CHANGES I WANT TO MAKE FOR TOMORROW:

_____

_____

_____

RECORD

GOALS FOR TODAY:

☐ _____
☐ _____
☐ _____

TO-DOS THAT CAN WAIT:

☐ _____
☐ _____
☐ _____

I'M EXCITED ABOUT:

_____
_____
_____

I'M STRESSED ABOUT:

_____
_____
_____

HOW I SPENT MY TIME (HOURS/MINUTES):

SLEEPING: _____   WORKING: _____

ON A SCREEN: _____   EATING: _____

EXERCISING: _____   FOR MYSELF: _____

PLAYING: _____   WITH FAMILY: _____

BEING CREATIVE: _____   SOCIALIZING: _____

RELAXING: _____   OTHER: _____

FOOD/DRINK I CONSUMED TODAY:

BREAKFAST   LUNCH   DINNER

_____   _____   _____
_____   _____   _____
_____   _____   _____

WATER/CAFFEINE (GLASSES/CUPS): 1   2   3   4   5   6   7   8

REFLECT

RATE YOUR ENERGY LEVEL TODAY:

1   2   3   4   5   6   7   8   9   10

MY ENERGY LEVEL WAS HIGHEST IN THE:

MORNING   AFTERNOON   EVENING

WHAT RECHARGED ME TODAY:

☐ TAKING A BATH   ☐ JOURNALING   ☐ BEING CREATIVE
☐ TAKING A NAP   ☐ SEEING A FRIEND   ☐ UNPLUGGING
☐ WALKING   ☐ TIME ALONE   ☐ TIME WITH FAMILY
☐ WORKING OUT   ☐ LISTENING TO   ☐ WHAT I ATE
☐ STRETCHING   MUSIC   ☐ OTHER: _____

THIS RECHARGED ME THE MOST TODAY:

_____
_____
_____

THOUGHTS I NEED TO CLEAR TO RELAX:

_____
_____
_____

CHANGES I WANT TO MAKE FOR TOMORROW:

_____
_____
_____

RECORD

GOALS FOR TODAY:

☐ _____
☐ _____
☐ _____

TO-DOS THAT CAN WAIT:

☐ _____
☐ _____
☐ _____

I'M EXCITED ABOUT:

_____
_____
_____

I'M STRESSED ABOUT:

_____
_____
_____

HOW I SPENT MY TIME (HOURS/MINUTES):

SLEEPING: _____   WORKING: _____

ON A SCREEN: _____   EATING: _____

EXERCISING: _____   FOR MYSELF: _____

PLAYING: _____   WITH FAMILY: _____

BEING CREATIVE: _____ SOCIALIZING: _____

RELAXING: _____   OTHER: _____

FOOD/DRINK I CONSUMED TODAY:

BREAKFAST   LUNCH   DINNER

_____   _____   _____
_____   _____   _____
_____   _____   _____

WATER/CAFFEINE (GLASSES/CUPS):   1   2   3   4   5   6   7   8

REFLECT

RATE YOUR ENERGY LEVEL TODAY:

1   2   3   4   5   6   7   8   9   10

MY ENERGY LEVEL WAS HIGHEST IN THE:

MORNING   AFTERNOON   EVENING

WHAT RECHARGED ME TODAY:

- [ ] TAKING A BATH
- [ ] TAKING A NAP
- [ ] WALKING
- [ ] WORKING OUT
- [ ] STRETCHING

- [ ] JOURNALING
- [ ] SEEING A FRIEND
- [ ] TIME ALONE
- [ ] LISTENING TO MUSIC

- [ ] BEING CREATIVE
- [ ] UNPLUGGING
- [ ] TIME WITH FAMILY
- [ ] WHAT I ATE
- [ ] OTHER: _____

THIS RECHARGED ME THE MOST TODAY:

_____
_____
_____

THOUGHTS I NEED TO CLEAR TO RELAX:

_____
_____
_____

CHANGES I WANT TO MAKE FOR TOMORROW:

_____
_____
_____

RECORD

DATE ___/___/___

GOALS FOR TODAY:

☐ —————————————————
☐ —————————————————
☐ —————————————————

TO-DOS THAT CAN WAIT:

☐ —————————————————
☐ —————————————————
☐ —————————————————

I'M EXCITED ABOUT:

—————————————————
—————————————————
—————————————————

I'M STRESSED ABOUT:

—————————————————
—————————————————
—————————————————

HOW I SPENT MY TIME (HOURS/MINUTES):

SLEEPING: _____

ON A SCREEN: _____

EXERCISING: _____

PLAYING: _____

BEING CREATIVE: _____

RELAXING: _____

WORKING: _____

EATING: _____

FOR MYSELF: _____

WITH FAMILY: _____

SOCIALIZING: _____

OTHER: _____

FOOD/DRINK I CONSUMED TODAY:

BREAKFAST

—————————————
—————————————
—————————————

LUNCH

—————————————
—————————————
—————————————

DINNER

—————————————
—————————————
—————————————

WATER/CAFFEINE (GLASSES/CUPS): 1 2 3 4 5 6 7 8

REFLECT

RATE YOUR ENERGY LEVEL TODAY:

1   2   3   4   5   6   7   8   9   10

MY ENERGY LEVEL WAS HIGHEST IN THE:

MORNING   AFTERNOON   EVENING

WHAT RECHARGED ME TODAY:

- [ ] TAKING A BATH
- [ ] TAKING A NAP
- [ ] WALKING
- [ ] WORKING OUT
- [ ] STRETCHING
- [ ] JOURNALING
- [ ] SEEING A FRIEND
- [ ] TIME ALONE
- [ ] LISTENING TO MUSIC
- [ ] BEING CREATIVE
- [ ] UNPLUGGING
- [ ] TIME WITH FAMILY
- [ ] WHAT I ATE
- [ ] OTHER: _____

THIS RECHARGED ME THE MOST TODAY:

_____

_____

_____

THOUGHTS I NEED TO CLEAR TO RELAX:

_____

_____

_____

CHANGES I WANT TO MAKE FOR TOMORROW:

_____

_____

_____

RECORD

DATE ___/___/___

GOALS FOR TODAY:

☐ ——————————————
☐ ——————————————
☐ ——————————————

TO-DOS THAT CAN WAIT:

☐ ——————————————
☐ ——————————————
☐ ——————————————

I'M EXCITED ABOUT:

——————————————————
——————————————————
——————————————————

I'M STRESSED ABOUT:

——————————————————
——————————————————
——————————————————

HOW I SPENT MY TIME (HOURS/MINUTES):

SLEEPING: _____

ON A SCREEN:_____

EXERCISING:_____

PLAYING: _____

BEING CREATIVE:_____

RELAXING: _____

WORKING:_____

EATING: _____

FOR MYSELF: _____

WITH FAMILY: _____

SOCIALIZING: _____

OTHER:_____

FOOD/DRINK I CONSUMED TODAY:

BREAKFAST

——————————
——————————
——————————

LUNCH

——————————
——————————
——————————

DINNER

——————————
——————————
——————————

WATER/CAFFEINE (GLASSES/CUPS): 1   2   3   4   5   6   7   8

REFLECT

RATE YOUR ENERGY LEVEL TODAY:

1   2   3   4   5   6   7   8   9   10

MY ENERGY LEVEL WAS HIGHEST IN THE:

MORNING   AFTERNOON   EVENING

WHAT RECHARGED ME TODAY:

- [ ] TAKING A BATH
- [ ] TAKING A NAP
- [ ] WALKING
- [ ] WORKING OUT
- [ ] STRETCHING

- [ ] JOURNALING
- [ ] SEEING A FRIEND
- [ ] TIME ALONE
- [ ] LISTENING TO
      MUSIC

- [ ] BEING CREATIVE
- [ ] UNPLUGGING
- [ ] TIME WITH FAMILY
- [ ] WHAT I ATE
- [ ] OTHER:_____

THIS RECHARGED ME THE MOST TODAY:

_____

_____

_____

THOUGHTS I NEED TO CLEAR TO RELAX:

_____

_____

_____

CHANGES I WANT TO MAKE FOR TOMORROW:

_____

_____

_____

RECORD

DATE ___/___/___

GOALS FOR TODAY:

☐ ————————————
☐ ————————————
☐ ————————————

TO-DOS THAT CAN WAIT:

☐ ————————————
☐ ————————————
☐ ————————————

I'M EXCITED ABOUT:

————————————
————————————
————————————

I'M STRESSED ABOUT:

————————————
————————————
————————————

HOW I SPENT MY TIME (HOURS/MINUTES):

SLEEPING:_____

ON A SCREEN:_____

EXERCISING:_____

PLAYING: _____

BEING CREATIVE:_____

RELAXING: _____

WORKING:_____

EATING: _____

FOR MYSELF: _____

WITH FAMILY: _____

SOCIALIZING: _____

OTHER:_____

FOOD/DRINK I CONSUMED TODAY:

BREAKFAST

————————————
————————————
————————————

LUNCH

————————————
————————————
————————————

DINNER

————————————
————————————
————————————

WATER/CAFFEINE (GLASSES/CUPS):   1   2   3   4   5   6   7   8

REFLECT

RATE YOUR ENERGY LEVEL TODAY:

1   2   3   4   5   6   7   8   9   10

MY ENERGY LEVEL WAS HIGHEST IN THE:

MORNING   AFTERNOON   EVENING

WHAT RECHARGED ME TODAY:

☐ TAKING A BATH   ☐ JOURNALING   ☐ BEING CREATIVE
☐ TAKING A NAP   ☐ SEEING A FRIEND   ☐ UNPLUGGING
☐ WALKING   ☐ TIME ALONE   ☐ TIME WITH FAMILY
☐ WORKING OUT   ☐ LISTENING TO   ☐ WHAT I ATE
☐ STRETCHING   MUSIC   ☐ OTHER: _____

THIS RECHARGED ME THE MOST TODAY:

_____
_____
_____

THOUGHTS I NEED TO CLEAR TO RELAX:

_____
_____
_____

CHANGES I WANT TO MAKE FOR TOMORROW:

_____
_____
_____

RECORD

DATE ___/___/___

GOALS FOR TODAY:

☐ _____
☐ _____
☐ _____

TO-DOS THAT CAN WAIT:

☐ _____
☐ _____
☐ _____

I'M EXCITED ABOUT:

_____
_____
_____

I'M STRESSED ABOUT:

_____
_____
_____

HOW I SPENT MY TIME (HOURS/MINUTES):

SLEEPING: _____

ON A SCREEN: _____

EXERCISING: _____

PLAYING: _____

BEING CREATIVE: _____

RELAXING: _____

WORKING: _____

EATING: _____

FOR MYSELF: _____

WITH FAMILY: _____

SOCIALIZING: _____

OTHER: _____

FOOD/DRINK I CONSUMED TODAY:

BREAKFAST

_____
_____
_____

LUNCH

_____
_____
_____

DINNER

_____
_____
_____

WATER/CAFFEINE (GLASSES/CUPS):   1   2   3   4   5   6   7   8

REFLECT

RATE YOUR ENERGY LEVEL TODAY:

1   2   3   4   5   6   7   8   9   10

MY ENERGY LEVEL WAS HIGHEST IN THE:

MORNING   AFTERNOON   EVENING

WHAT RECHARGED ME TODAY:

☐ TAKING A BATH   ☐ JOURNALING   ☐ BEING CREATIVE
☐ TAKING A NAP   ☐ SEEING A FRIEND   ☐ UNPLUGGING
☐ WALKING   ☐ TIME ALONE   ☐ TIME WITH FAMILY
☐ WORKING OUT   ☐ LISTENING TO   ☐ WHAT I ATE
☐ STRETCHING   MUSIC   ☐ OTHER:_____

THIS RECHARGED ME THE MOST TODAY:

_____
_____
_____

THOUGHTS I NEED TO CLEAR TO RELAX:

_____
_____
_____

CHANGES I WANT TO MAKE FOR TOMORROW:

_____
_____
_____

RECORD

GOALS FOR TODAY:

☐ _____
☐ _____
☐ _____

TO-DOS THAT CAN WAIT:

☐ _____
☐ _____
☐ _____

I'M EXCITED ABOUT:

_____
_____
_____

I'M STRESSED ABOUT:

_____
_____
_____

HOW I SPENT MY TIME (HOURS/MINUTES):

SLEEPING: _____   WORKING: _____

ON A SCREEN: _____   EATING: _____

EXERCISING: _____   FOR MYSELF: _____

PLAYING: _____   WITH FAMILY: _____

BEING CREATIVE: _____   SOCIALIZING: _____

RELAXING: _____   OTHER: _____

FOOD/DRINK I CONSUMED TODAY:

BREAKFAST   LUNCH   DINNER

_____   _____   _____
_____   _____   _____
_____   _____   _____

WATER/CAFFEINE (GLASSES/CUPS): 1   2   3   4   5   6   7   8

REFLECT

RATE YOUR ENERGY LEVEL TODAY:

1   2   3   4   5   6   7   8   9   10

MY ENERGY LEVEL WAS HIGHEST IN THE:

MORNING   AFTERNOON   EVENING

WHAT RECHARGED ME TODAY:

- [ ] TAKING A BATH
- [ ] TAKING A NAP
- [ ] WALKING
- [ ] WORKING OUT
- [ ] STRETCHING

- [ ] JOURNALING
- [ ] SEEING A FRIEND
- [ ] TIME ALONE
- [ ] LISTENING TO
  MUSIC

- [ ] BEING CREATIVE
- [ ] UNPLUGGING
- [ ] TIME WITH FAMILY
- [ ] WHAT I ATE
- [ ] OTHER: _____

THIS RECHARGED ME THE MOST TODAY:

_____

_____

_____

THOUGHTS I NEED TO CLEAR TO RELAX:

_____

_____

_____

CHANGES I WANT TO MAKE FOR TOMORROW:

_____

_____

_____

RECORD

DATE ___/___/___

GOALS FOR TODAY:

☐ _____
☐ _____
☐ _____

TO-DOS THAT CAN WAIT:

☐ _____
☐ _____
☐ _____

I'M EXCITED ABOUT:

_____
_____
_____

I'M STRESSED ABOUT:

_____
_____
_____

HOW I SPENT MY TIME (HOURS/MINUTES):

SLEEPING: _____

ON A SCREEN: _____

EXERCISING: _____

PLAYING: _____

BEING CREATIVE: _____

RELAXING: _____

WORKING: _____

EATING: _____

FOR MYSELF: _____

WITH FAMILY: _____

SOCIALIZING: _____

OTHER: _____

FOOD/DRINK I CONSUMED TODAY:

BREAKFAST

_____
_____
_____

LUNCH

_____
_____
_____

DINNER

_____
_____
_____

WATER/CAFFEINE (GLASSES/CUPS): 1   2   3   4   5   6   7   8

REFLECT

RATE YOUR ENERGY LEVEL TODAY:

1   2   3   4   5   6   7   8   9   10

MY ENERGY LEVEL WAS HIGHEST IN THE:

MORNING   AFTERNOON   EVENING

WHAT RECHARGED ME TODAY:

- [ ] TAKING A BATH
- [ ] TAKING A NAP
- [ ] WALKING
- [ ] WORKING OUT
- [ ] STRETCHING

- [ ] JOURNALING
- [ ] SEEING A FRIEND
- [ ] TIME ALONE
- [ ] LISTENING TO
      MUSIC

- [ ] BEING CREATIVE
- [ ] UNPLUGGING
- [ ] TIME WITH FAMILY
- [ ] WHAT I ATE
- [ ] OTHER: _____

THIS RECHARGED ME THE MOST TODAY:

_____

_____

_____

THOUGHTS I NEED TO CLEAR TO RELAX:

_____

_____

_____

CHANGES I WANT TO MAKE FOR TOMORROW:

_____

_____

_____

RECORD

DATE ___/___/___

GOALS FOR TODAY:

☐ _____
☐ _____
☐ _____

TO-DOS THAT CAN WAIT:

☐ _____
☐ _____
☐ _____

I'M EXCITED ABOUT:

_____
_____
_____

I'M STRESSED ABOUT:

_____
_____
_____

HOW I SPENT MY TIME (HOURS/MINUTES):

SLEEPING: _____

ON A SCREEN: _____

EXERCISING: _____

PLAYING: _____

BEING CREATIVE: _____

RELAXING: _____

WORKING: _____

EATING: _____

FOR MYSELF: _____

WITH FAMILY: _____

SOCIALIZING: _____

OTHER: _____

FOOD/DRINK I CONSUMED TODAY:

BREAKFAST

_____
_____
_____

LUNCH

_____
_____
_____

DINNER

_____
_____
_____

WATER/CAFFEINE (GLASSES/CUPS): 1   2   3   4   5   6   7   8

REFLECT

RATE YOUR ENERGY LEVEL TODAY:

1   2   3   4   5   6   7   8   9   10

MY ENERGY LEVEL WAS HIGHEST IN THE:

MORNING   AFTERNOON   EVENING

WHAT RECHARGED ME TODAY:

- ☐ TAKING A BATH
- ☐ TAKING A NAP
- ☐ WALKING
- ☐ WORKING OUT
- ☐ STRETCHING

- ☐ JOURNALING
- ☐ SEEING A FRIEND
- ☐ TIME ALONE
- ☐ LISTENING TO
  MUSIC

- ☐ BEING CREATIVE
- ☐ UNPLUGGING
- ☐ TIME WITH FAMILY
- ☐ WHAT I ATE
- ☐ OTHER: _____

THIS RECHARGED ME THE MOST TODAY:

_____

_____

_____

THOUGHTS I NEED TO CLEAR TO RELAX:

_____

_____

_____

CHANGES I WANT TO MAKE FOR TOMORROW:

_____

_____

_____

RECORD

DATE ____/____/____

GOALS FOR TODAY:

☐ _____
☐ _____
☐ _____

TO-DOS THAT CAN WAIT:

☐ _____
☐ _____
☐ _____

I'M EXCITED ABOUT:

_____
_____
_____

I'M STRESSED ABOUT:

_____
_____
_____

HOW I SPENT MY TIME (HOURS/MINUTES):

SLEEPING:_____

ON A SCREEN:_____

EXERCISING:_____

PLAYING: _____

BEING CREATIVE:_____

RELAXING: _____

WORKING:_____

EATING: _____

FOR MYSELF:_____

WITH FAMILY: _____

SOCIALIZING:_____

OTHER:_____

FOOD/DRINK I CONSUMED TODAY:

BREAKFAST

_____
_____
_____

LUNCH

_____
_____
_____

DINNER

_____
_____
_____

WATER/CAFFEINE (GLASSES/CUPS): 1   2   3   4   5   6   7   8

REFLECT

RATE YOUR ENERGY LEVEL TODAY:

1   2   3   4   5   6   7   8   9   10

MY ENERGY LEVEL WAS HIGHEST IN THE:
MORNING   AFTERNOON   EVENING

WHAT RECHARGED ME TODAY:

☐ TAKING A BATH   ☐ JOURNALING   ☐ BEING CREATIVE
☐ TAKING A NAP   ☐ SEEING A FRIEND ☐ UNPLUGGING
☐ WALKING   ☐ TIME ALONE   ☐ TIME WITH FAMILY
☐ WORKING OUT   ☐ LISTENING TO   ☐ WHAT I ATE
☐ STRETCHING   MUSIC   ☐ OTHER:_____

THIS RECHARGED ME THE MOST TODAY:
_____
_____
_____

THOUGHTS I NEED TO CLEAR TO RELAX:
_____
_____
_____

CHANGES I WANT TO MAKE FOR TOMORROW:
_____
_____
_____

RECORD

DATE ___/___/___

GOALS FOR TODAY:

☐ _____
☐ _____
☐ _____

TO-DOS THAT CAN WAIT:

☐ _____
☐ _____
☐ _____

I'M EXCITED ABOUT:

_____
_____
_____

I'M STRESSED ABOUT:

_____
_____
_____

HOW I SPENT MY TIME (HOURS/MINUTES):

SLEEPING: _____

ON A SCREEN: _____

EXERCISING: _____

PLAYING: _____

BEING CREATIVE: _____

RELAXING: _____

WORKING: _____

EATING: _____

FOR MYSELF: _____

WITH FAMILY: _____

SOCIALIZING: _____

OTHER: _____

FOOD/DRINK I CONSUMED TODAY:

BREAKFAST

_____
_____
_____

LUNCH

_____
_____
_____

DINNER

_____
_____
_____

WATER/CAFFEINE (GLASSES/CUPS):   1   2   3   4   5   6   7   8

REFLECT

RATE YOUR ENERGY LEVEL TODAY:

1   2   3   4   5   6   7   8   9   10

MY ENERGY LEVEL WAS HIGHEST IN THE:

MORNING   AFTERNOON   EVENING

WHAT RECHARGED ME TODAY:

☐ TAKING A BATH   ☐ JOURNALING   ☐ BEING CREATIVE
☐ TAKING A NAP   ☐ SEEING A FRIEND ☐ UNPLUGGING
☐ WALKING   ☐ TIME ALONE   ☐ TIME WITH FAMILY
☐ WORKING OUT   ☐ LISTENING TO   ☐ WHAT I ATE
☐ STRETCHING   MUSIC   ☐ OTHER: _____

THIS RECHARGED ME THE MOST TODAY:

_____

_____

_____

THOUGHTS I NEED TO CLEAR TO RELAX:

_____

_____

_____

CHANGES I WANT TO MAKE FOR TOMORROW:

_____

_____

_____

RECORD

DATE ___/___/___

GOALS FOR TODAY:

☐ _____
☐ _____
☐ _____

TO-DOS THAT CAN WAIT:

☐ _____
☐ _____
☐ _____

I'M EXCITED ABOUT:

_____
_____
_____

I'M STRESSED ABOUT:

_____
_____
_____

HOW I SPENT MY TIME (HOURS/MINUTES):

SLEEPING:_____

ON A SCREEN:_____

EXERCISING:_____

PLAYING: _____

BEING CREATIVE:_____

RELAXING: _____

WORKING:_____

EATING: _____

FOR MYSELF: _____

WITH FAMILY: _____

SOCIALIZING: _____

OTHER:_____

FOOD/DRINK I CONSUMED TODAY:

BREAKFAST

_____
_____
_____

LUNCH

_____
_____
_____

DINNER

_____
_____
_____

WATER/CAFFEINE (GLASSES/CUPS): 1   2   3   4   5   6   7   8

REFLECT

RATE YOUR ENERGY LEVEL TODAY:

1   2   3   4   5   6   7   8   9   10

MY ENERGY LEVEL WAS HIGHEST IN THE:

MORNING   AFTERNOON   EVENING

WHAT RECHARGED ME TODAY:

- [ ] TAKING A BATH
- [ ] TAKING A NAP
- [ ] WALKING
- [ ] WORKING OUT
- [ ] STRETCHING

- [ ] JOURNALING
- [ ] SEEING A FRIEND
- [ ] TIME ALONE
- [ ] LISTENING TO
      MUSIC

- [ ] BEING CREATIVE
- [ ] UNPLUGGING
- [ ] TIME WITH FAMILY
- [ ] WHAT I ATE
- [ ] OTHER: _____

THIS RECHARGED ME THE MOST TODAY:

_____
_____
_____

THOUGHTS I NEED TO CLEAR TO RELAX:

_____
_____
_____

CHANGES I WANT TO MAKE FOR TOMORROW:

_____
_____
_____

RECORD

DATE ___ / ___ / ___

GOALS FOR TODAY:

- ☐ _____
- ☐ _____
- ☐ _____

TO-DOS THAT CAN WAIT:

- ☐ _____
- ☐ _____
- ☐ _____

I'M EXCITED ABOUT:

_____
_____
_____

I'M STRESSED ABOUT:

_____
_____
_____

HOW I SPENT MY TIME (HOURS/MINUTES):

SLEEPING: _____

ON A SCREEN: _____

EXERCISING: _____

PLAYING: _____

BEING CREATIVE: _____

RELAXING: _____

WORKING: _____

EATING: _____

FOR MYSELF: _____

WITH FAMILY: _____

SOCIALIZING: _____

OTHER: _____

FOOD/DRINK I CONSUMED TODAY:

BREAKFAST

_____
_____
_____

LUNCH

_____
_____
_____

DINNER

_____
_____
_____

WATER/CAFFEINE (GLASSES/CUPS): 1   2   3   4   5   6   7   8

REFLECT

RATE YOUR ENERGY LEVEL TODAY:

1   2   3   4   5   6   7   8   9   10

MY ENERGY LEVEL WAS HIGHEST IN THE:

MORNING   AFTERNOON   EVENING

WHAT RECHARGED ME TODAY:

- [ ] TAKING A BATH
- [ ] TAKING A NAP
- [ ] WALKING
- [ ] WORKING OUT
- [ ] STRETCHING

- [ ] JOURNALING
- [ ] SEEING A FRIEND
- [ ] TIME ALONE
- [ ] LISTENING TO
      MUSIC

- [ ] BEING CREATIVE
- [ ] UNPLUGGING
- [ ] TIME WITH FAMILY
- [ ] WHAT I ATE
- [ ] OTHER:_____

THIS RECHARGED ME THE MOST TODAY:

_____
_____
_____

THOUGHTS I NEED TO CLEAR TO RELAX:

_____
_____
_____

CHANGES I WANT TO MAKE FOR TOMORROW:

_____
_____
_____

RECORD

DATE ___/___/___

GOALS FOR TODAY:

☐ _____
☐ _____
☐ _____

TO-DOS THAT CAN WAIT:

☐ _____
☐ _____
☐ _____

I'M EXCITED ABOUT:

_____
_____
_____

I'M STRESSED ABOUT:

_____
_____
_____

HOW I SPENT MY TIME (HOURS/MINUTES):

SLEEPING: _____

ON A SCREEN: _____

EXERCISING: _____

PLAYING: _____

BEING CREATIVE: _____

RELAXING: _____

WORKING: _____

EATING: _____

FOR MYSELF: _____

WITH FAMILY: _____

SOCIALIZING: _____

OTHER: _____

FOOD/DRINK I CONSUMED TODAY:

BREAKFAST

_____
_____
_____

LUNCH

_____
_____
_____

DINNER

_____
_____
_____

WATER/CAFFEINE (GLASSES/CUPS):   1   2   3   4   5   6   7   8

REFLECT

RATE YOUR ENERGY LEVEL TODAY:

1   2   3   4   5   6   7   8   9   10

MY ENERGY LEVEL WAS HIGHEST IN THE:

MORNING   AFTERNOON   EVENING

WHAT RECHARGED ME TODAY:

☐ TAKING A BATH   ☐ JOURNALING   ☐ BEING CREATIVE
☐ TAKING A NAP   ☐ SEEING A FRIEND ☐ UNPLUGGING
☐ WALKING   ☐ TIME ALONE   ☐ TIME WITH FAMILY
☐ WORKING OUT   ☐ LISTENING TO   ☐ WHAT I ATE
☐ STRETCHING   MUSIC   ☐ OTHER:_____

THIS RECHARGED ME THE MOST TODAY:

_____

_____

_____

THOUGHTS I NEED TO CLEAR TO RELAX:

_____

_____

_____

CHANGES I WANT TO MAKE FOR TOMORROW:

_____

_____

RECORD

DATE ___ / ___ / ___

GOALS FOR TODAY:

☐ _____
☐ _____
☐ _____

TO-DOS THAT CAN WAIT:

☐ _____
☐ _____
☐ _____

I'M EXCITED ABOUT:

_____
_____
_____

I'M STRESSED ABOUT:

_____
_____
_____

HOW I SPENT MY TIME (HOURS/MINUTES):

SLEEPING: _____
ON A SCREEN: _____
EXERCISING: _____
PLAYING: _____
BEING CREATIVE: _____
RELAXING: _____

WORKING: _____
EATING: _____
FOR MYSELF: _____
WITH FAMILY: _____
SOCIALIZING: _____
OTHER: _____

FOOD/DRINK I CONSUMED TODAY:

BREAKFAST

_____
_____
_____

LUNCH

_____
_____
_____

DINNER

_____
_____
_____

WATER/CAFFEINE (GLASSES/CUPS): 1 2 3 4 5 6 7 8

REFLECT

RATE YOUR ENERGY LEVEL TODAY:

1   2   3   4   5   6   7   8   9   10

MY ENERGY LEVEL WAS HIGHEST IN THE:

MORNING   AFTERNOON   EVENING

WHAT RECHARGED ME TODAY:

- [ ] TAKING A BATH
- [ ] TAKING A NAP
- [ ] WALKING
- [ ] WORKING OUT
- [ ] STRETCHING

- [ ] JOURNALING
- [ ] SEEING A FRIEND
- [ ] TIME ALONE
- [ ] LISTENING TO
      MUSIC

- [ ] BEING CREATIVE
- [ ] UNPLUGGING
- [ ] TIME WITH FAMILY
- [ ] WHAT I ATE
- [ ] OTHER: _____

THIS RECHARGED ME THE MOST TODAY:

_____

_____

_____

THOUGHTS I NEED TO CLEAR TO RELAX:

_____

_____

_____

CHANGES I WANT TO MAKE FOR TOMORROW:

_____

_____

_____

RECORD

DATE ___/___/___

GOALS FOR TODAY:

☐ —————————————————
☐ —————————————————
☐ —————————————————

TO-DOS THAT CAN WAIT:

☐ —————————————————
☐ —————————————————
☐ —————————————————

I'M EXCITED ABOUT:

————————————————————
————————————————————
————————————————————

I'M STRESSED ABOUT:

————————————————————
————————————————————
————————————————————

HOW I SPENT MY TIME (HOURS/MINUTES):

SLEEPING:_____

ON A SCREEN:_____

EXERCISING:_____

PLAYING: _____

BEING CREATIVE:_____

RELAXING: _____

WORKING:_____

EATING: _____

FOR MYSELF: _____

WITH FAMILY: _____

SOCIALIZING: _____

OTHER:_____

FOOD/DRINK I CONSUMED TODAY:

BREAKFAST

————————————————
————————————————
————————————————

LUNCH

————————————————
————————————————
————————————————

DINNER

————————————————
————————————————
————————————————

WATER/CAFFEINE (GLASSES/CUPS): 1   2   3   4   5   6   7   8

REFLECT

RATE YOUR ENERGY LEVEL TODAY:

1   2   3   4   5   6   7   8   9   10

MY ENERGY LEVEL WAS HIGHEST IN THE:

MORNING   AFTERNOON   EVENING

WHAT RECHARGED ME TODAY:

☐ TAKING A BATH   ☐ JOURNALING   ☐ BEING CREATIVE
☐ TAKING A NAP   ☐ SEEING A FRIEND   ☐ UNPLUGGING
☐ WALKING   ☐ TIME ALONE   ☐ TIME WITH FAMILY
☐ WORKING OUT   ☐ LISTENING TO   ☐ WHAT I ATE
☐ STRETCHING   MUSIC   ☐ OTHER:_____

THIS RECHARGED ME THE MOST TODAY:

_____
_____
_____

THOUGHTS I NEED TO CLEAR TO RELAX:

_____
_____
_____

CHANGES I WANT TO MAKE FOR TOMORROW:

_____
_____
_____

RECORD

DATE ___/___/___

GOALS FOR TODAY:

☐ _____'
☐ _____
☐ _____

TO-DOS THAT CAN WAIT:

☐ _____
☐ _____
☐ _____

I'M EXCITED ABOUT:

_____
_____
_____

I'M STRESSED ABOUT:

_____
_____
_____

HOW I SPENT MY TIME (HOURS/MINUTES):

SLEEPING: _____
ON A SCREEN: _____
EXERCISING: _____
PLAYING: _____
BEING CREATIVE: _____
RELAXING: _____

WORKING: _____
EATING: _____
FOR MYSELF: _____
WITH FAMILY: _____
SOCIALIZING: _____
OTHER: _____

FOOD/DRINK I CONSUMED TODAY:

BREAKFAST

_____
_____
_____

LUNCH

_____
_____
_____

DINNER

_____
_____
_____

WATER/CAFFEINE (GLASSES/CUPS): 1   2   3   4   5   6   7   8

REFLECT

RATE YOUR ENERGY LEVEL TODAY:

1   2   3   4   5   6   7   8   9   10

MY ENERGY LEVEL WAS HIGHEST IN THE:

MORNING   AFTERNOON   EVENING

WHAT RECHARGED ME TODAY:

- [ ] TAKING A BATH
- [ ] TAKING A NAP
- [ ] WALKING
- [ ] WORKING OUT
- [ ] STRETCHING

- [ ] JOURNALING
- [ ] SEEING A FRIEND
- [ ] TIME ALONE
- [ ] LISTENING TO MUSIC

- [ ] BEING CREATIVE
- [ ] UNPLUGGING
- [ ] TIME WITH FAMILY
- [ ] WHAT I ATE
- [ ] OTHER:_____

THIS RECHARGED ME THE MOST TODAY:

_____

_____

_____

THOUGHTS I NEED TO CLEAR TO RELAX:

_____

_____

_____

CHANGES I WANT TO MAKE FOR TOMORROW:

_____

_____

_____

RECORD

DATE ___/___/___

GOALS FOR TODAY:

☐ _____
☐ _____
☐ _____

TO-DOS THAT CAN WAIT:

☐ _____
☐ _____
☐ _____

I'M EXCITED ABOUT:

_____
_____
_____

I'M STRESSED ABOUT:

_____
_____
_____

HOW I SPENT MY TIME (HOURS/MINUTES):

SLEEPING: _____
ON A SCREEN: _____
EXERCISING: _____
PLAYING: _____
BEING CREATIVE: _____
RELAXING: _____

WORKING: _____
EATING: _____
FOR MYSELF: _____
WITH FAMILY: _____
SOCIALIZING: _____
OTHER: _____

FOOD/DRINK I CONSUMED TODAY:

BREAKFAST

_____
_____
_____

LUNCH

_____
_____
_____

DINNER

_____
_____
_____

WATER/CAFFEINE (GLASSES/CUPS): 1   2   3   4   5   6   7   8

REFLECT

RATE YOUR ENERGY LEVEL TODAY:

1   2   3   4   5   6   7   8   9   10

MY ENERGY LEVEL WAS HIGHEST IN THE:

MORNING   AFTERNOON   EVENING

WHAT RECHARGED ME TODAY:

- [ ] TAKING A BATH
- [ ] TAKING A NAP
- [ ] WALKING
- [ ] WORKING OUT
- [ ] STRETCHING

- [ ] JOURNALING
- [ ] SEEING A FRIEND
- [ ] TIME ALONE
- [ ] LISTENING TO
  MUSIC

- [ ] BEING CREATIVE
- [ ] UNPLUGGING
- [ ] TIME WITH FAMILY
- [ ] WHAT I ATE
- [ ] OTHER: _____

THIS RECHARGED ME THE MOST TODAY:

_____

_____

_____

THOUGHTS I NEED TO CLEAR TO RELAX:

_____

_____

_____

CHANGES I WANT TO MAKE FOR TOMORROW:

_____

_____

_____

RECORD

DATE ___/___/___

GOALS FOR TODAY:

☐ _____
☐ _____
☐ _____

TO-DOS THAT CAN WAIT:

☐ _____
☐ _____
☐ _____

I'M EXCITED ABOUT:

_____
_____
_____

I'M STRESSED ABOUT:

_____
_____
_____

HOW I SPENT MY TIME (HOURS/MINUTES):

SLEEPING: _____
ON A SCREEN: _____
EXERCISING: _____
PLAYING: _____
BEING CREATIVE: _____
RELAXING: _____

WORKING: _____
EATING: _____
FOR MYSELF: _____
WITH FAMILY: _____
SOCIALIZING: _____
OTHER: _____

FOOD/DRINK I CONSUMED TODAY:

BREAKFAST
_____
_____
_____

LUNCH
_____
_____
_____

DINNER
_____
_____
_____

WATER/CAFFEINE (GLASSES/CUPS):   1   2   3   4   5   6   7   8

REFLECT

RATE YOUR ENERGY LEVEL TODAY:

1   2   3   4   5   6   7   8   9   10

MY ENERGY LEVEL WAS HIGHEST IN THE:

MORNING   AFTERNOON   EVENING

WHAT RECHARGED ME TODAY:

- [ ] TAKING A BATH
- [ ] TAKING A NAP
- [ ] WALKING
- [ ] WORKING OUT
- [ ] STRETCHING

- [ ] JOURNALING
- [ ] SEEING A FRIEND
- [ ] TIME ALONE
- [ ] LISTENING TO MUSIC

- [ ] BEING CREATIVE
- [ ] UNPLUGGING
- [ ] TIME WITH FAMILY
- [ ] WHAT I ATE
- [ ] OTHER: _____

THIS RECHARGED ME THE MOST TODAY:

_____
_____
_____

THOUGHTS I NEED TO CLEAR TO RELAX:

_____
_____
_____

CHANGES I WANT TO MAKE FOR TOMORROW:

_____
_____
_____

RECORD

DATE ___/___/___

GOALS FOR TODAY:

☐ _____
☐ _____
☐ _____

TO-DOS THAT CAN WAIT:

☐ _____
☐ _____
☐ _____

I'M EXCITED ABOUT:

_____
_____
_____

I'M STRESSED ABOUT:

_____
_____
_____

HOW I SPENT MY TIME (HOURS/MINUTES):

SLEEPING: _____

ON A SCREEN: _____

EXERCISING: _____

PLAYING: _____

BEING CREATIVE: _____

RELAXING: _____

WORKING: _____

EATING: _____

FOR MYSELF: _____

WITH FAMILY: _____

SOCIALIZING: _____

OTHER: _____

FOOD/DRINK I CONSUMED TODAY:

BREAKFAST

_____
_____
_____

LUNCH

_____
_____
_____

DINNER

_____
_____
_____

WATER/CAFFEINE (GLASSES/CUPS):   1   2   3   4   5   6   7   8

REFLECT

RATE YOUR ENERGY LEVEL TODAY:

1   2   3   4   5   6   7   8   9   10

MY ENERGY LEVEL WAS HIGHEST IN THE:

MORNING   AFTERNOON   EVENING

WHAT RECHARGED ME TODAY:

- [ ] TAKING A BATH
- [ ] TAKING A NAP
- [ ] WALKING
- [ ] WORKING OUT
- [ ] STRETCHING

- [ ] JOURNALING
- [ ] SEEING A FRIEND
- [ ] TIME ALONE
- [ ] LISTENING TO
      MUSIC

- [ ] BEING CREATIVE
- [ ] UNPLUGGING
- [ ] TIME WITH FAMILY
- [ ] WHAT I ATE
- [ ] OTHER:_____

THIS RECHARGED ME THE MOST TODAY:

_____

_____

_____

THOUGHTS I NEED TO CLEAR TO RELAX:

_____

_____

_____

CHANGES I WANT TO MAKE FOR TOMORROW:

_____

_____

_____

RECORD

DATE ___/___/___

GOALS FOR TODAY:

☐ _____
☐ _____
☐ _____

TO-DOS THAT CAN WAIT:

☐ _____
☐ _____
☐ _____

I'M EXCITED ABOUT:

_____
_____
_____

I'M STRESSED ABOUT:

_____
_____
_____

HOW I SPENT MY TIME (HOURS/MINUTES):

SLEEPING: _____

ON A SCREEN: _____

EXERCISING: _____

PLAYING: _____

BEING CREATIVE: _____

RELAXING: _____

WORKING: _____

EATING: _____

FOR MYSELF: _____

WITH FAMILY: _____

SOCIALIZING: _____

OTHER: _____

FOOD/DRINK I CONSUMED TODAY:

BREAKFAST

_____
_____
_____

LUNCH

_____
_____
_____

DINNER

_____
_____
_____

WATER/CAFFEINE (GLASSES/CUPS): 1 2 3 4 5 6 7 8

REFLECT

RATE YOUR ENERGY LEVEL TODAY:

1   2   3   4   5   6   7   8   9   10

MY ENERGY LEVEL WAS HIGHEST IN THE:

MORNING   AFTERNOON   EVENING

WHAT RECHARGED ME TODAY:

☐ TAKING A BATH   ☐ JOURNALING   ☐ BEING CREATIVE
☐ TAKING A NAP   ☐ SEEING A FRIEND   ☐ UNPLUGGING
☐ WALKING   ☐ TIME ALONE   ☐ TIME WITH FAMILY
☐ WORKING OUT   ☐ LISTENING TO   ☐ WHAT I ATE
☐ STRETCHING   MUSIC   ☐ OTHER:_____

THIS RECHARGED ME THE MOST TODAY:
_____
_____
_____

THOUGHTS I NEED TO CLEAR TO RELAX:
_____
_____
_____

CHANGES I WANT TO MAKE FOR TOMORROW:
_____
_____
_____

RECORD

DATE ___/___/___

GOALS FOR TODAY:

☐ _____
☐ _____
☐ _____

TO-DOS THAT CAN WAIT:

☐ _____
☐ _____
☐ _____

I'M EXCITED ABOUT:

_____
_____
_____

I'M STRESSED ABOUT:

_____
_____
_____

HOW I SPENT MY TIME (HOURS/MINUTES):

SLEEPING: _____

ON A SCREEN: _____

EXERCISING: _____

PLAYING: _____

BEING CREATIVE: _____

RELAXING: _____

WORKING: _____

EATING: _____

FOR MYSELF: _____

WITH FAMILY: _____

SOCIALIZING: _____

OTHER: _____

FOOD/DRINK I CONSUMED TODAY:

BREAKFAST

_____
_____
_____

LUNCH

_____
_____
_____

DINNER

_____
_____
_____

WATER/CAFFEINE (GLASSES/CUPS): 1   2   3   4   5   6   7   8

REFLECT

RATE YOUR ENERGY LEVEL TODAY:

1   2   3   4   5   6   7   8   9   10

MY ENERGY LEVEL WAS HIGHEST IN THE:

MORNING   AFTERNOON   EVENING

WHAT RECHARGED ME TODAY:

☐ TAKING A BATH   ☐ JOURNALING   ☐ BEING CREATIVE
☐ TAKING A NAP   ☐ SEEING A FRIEND   ☐ UNPLUGGING
☐ WALKING   ☐ TIME ALONE   ☐ TIME WITH FAMILY
☐ WORKING OUT   ☐ LISTENING TO   ☐ WHAT I ATE
☐ STRETCHING   MUSIC   ☐ OTHER:_____

THIS RECHARGED ME THE MOST TODAY:

_____

_____

_____

THOUGHTS I NEED TO CLEAR TO RELAX:

_____

_____

_____

CHANGES I WANT TO MAKE FOR TOMORROW:

_____

_____

_____

RECORD

DATE ___/___/___

GOALS FOR TODAY:

☐ _____

☐ _____

☐ _____

TO-DOS THAT CAN WAIT:

☐ _____

☐ _____

☐ _____

I'M EXCITED ABOUT:

_____

_____

_____

I'M STRESSED ABOUT:

_____

_____

_____

HOW I SPENT MY TIME (HOURS/MINUTES):

SLEEPING: _____   WORKING: _____

ON A SCREEN: _____   EATING: _____

EXERCISING: _____   FOR MYSELF: _____

PLAYING: _____   WITH FAMILY: _____

BEING CREATIVE: _____   SOCIALIZING: _____

RELAXING: _____   OTHER: _____

FOOD/DRINK I CONSUMED TODAY:

BREAKFAST   LUNCH   DINNER

_____   _____   _____

_____   _____   _____

_____   _____   _____

WATER/CAFFEINE (GLASSES/CUPS): 1   2   3   4   5   6   7   8

REFLECT

RATE YOUR ENERGY LEVEL TODAY:

1   2   3   4   5   6   7   8   9   10

MY ENERGY LEVEL WAS HIGHEST IN THE:

MORNING   AFTERNOON   EVENING

WHAT RECHARGED ME TODAY:

☐ TAKING A BATH   ☐ JOURNALING   ☐ BEING CREATIVE
☐ TAKING A NAP   ☐ SEEING A FRIEND   ☐ UNPLUGGING
☐ WALKING   ☐ TIME ALONE   ☐ TIME WITH FAMILY
☐ WORKING OUT   ☐ LISTENING TO   ☐ WHAT I ATE
☐ STRETCHING   MUSIC   ☐ OTHER:_____

THIS RECHARGED ME THE MOST TODAY:

_____
_____
_____

THOUGHTS I NEED TO CLEAR TO RELAX:

_____
_____
_____

CHANGES I WANT TO MAKE FOR TOMORROW:

_____
_____

RECORD

DATE ___/___/___

GOALS FOR TODAY:

☐ ——————————————
☐ ——————————————
☐ ——————————————

TO-DOS THAT CAN WAIT:

☐ ——————————————
☐ ——————————————
☐ ——————————————

I'M EXCITED ABOUT:

——————————————
——————————————
——————————————

I'M STRESSED ABOUT:

——————————————
——————————————
——————————————

HOW I SPENT MY TIME (HOURS/MINUTES):

SLEEPING:_____

ON A SCREEN:_____

EXERCISING:_____

PLAYING: _____

BEING CREATIVE:_____

RELAXING: _____

WORKING:_____

EATING: _____

FOR MYSELF:_____

WITH FAMILY:_____

SOCIALIZING:_____

OTHER:_____

FOOD/DRINK I CONSUMED TODAY:

BREAKFAST

——————————
——————————
——————————

LUNCH

——————————
——————————
——————————

DINNER

——————————
——————————
——————————

WATER/CAFFEINE (GLASSES/CUPS):   1   2   3   4   5   6   7   8

REFLECT

RATE YOUR ENERGY LEVEL TODAY:

1   2   3   4   5   6   7   8   9   10

MY ENERGY LEVEL WAS HIGHEST IN THE:

MORNING   AFTERNOON   EVENING

WHAT RECHARGED ME TODAY:

- [ ] TAKING A BATH
- [ ] TAKING A NAP
- [ ] WALKING
- [ ] WORKING OUT
- [ ] STRETCHING

- [ ] JOURNALING
- [ ] SEEING A FRIEND
- [ ] TIME ALONE
- [ ] LISTENING TO MUSIC

- [ ] BEING CREATIVE
- [ ] UNPLUGGING
- [ ] TIME WITH FAMILY
- [ ] WHAT I ATE
- [ ] OTHER: _____

THIS RECHARGED ME THE MOST TODAY:

_____

_____

_____

THOUGHTS I NEED TO CLEAR TO RELAX:

_____

_____

_____

CHANGES I WANT TO MAKE FOR TOMORROW:

_____

_____

_____

RECORD

DATE ___/___/___

GOALS FOR TODAY:

☐ _____
☐ _____
☐ _____

TO-DOS THAT CAN WAIT:

☐ _____
☐ _____
☐ _____

I'M EXCITED ABOUT:

_____
_____
_____

I'M STRESSED ABOUT:

_____
_____
_____

HOW I SPENT MY TIME (HOURS/MINUTES):

SLEEPING: _____

ON A SCREEN: _____

EXERCISING: _____

PLAYING: _____

BEING CREATIVE: _____

RELAXING: _____

WORKING: _____

EATING: _____

FOR MYSELF: _____

WITH FAMILY: _____

SOCIALIZING: _____

OTHER: _____

FOOD/DRINK I CONSUMED TODAY:

BREAKFAST

_____
_____
_____

LUNCH

_____
_____
_____

DINNER

_____
_____
_____

WATER/CAFFEINE (GLASSES/CUPS): 1   2   3   4   5   6   7   8

REFLECT

RATE YOUR ENERGY LEVEL TODAY:

1   2   3   4   5   6   7   8   9   10

MY ENERGY LEVEL WAS HIGHEST IN THE:

MORNING   AFTERNOON   EVENING

WHAT RECHARGED ME TODAY:

- ☐ TAKING A BATH
- ☐ TAKING A NAP
- ☐ WALKING
- ☐ WORKING OUT
- ☐ STRETCHING

- ☐ JOURNALING
- ☐ SEEING A FRIEND
- ☐ TIME ALONE
- ☐ LISTENING TO
  MUSIC

- ☐ BEING CREATIVE
- ☐ UNPLUGGING
- ☐ TIME WITH FAMILY
- ☐ WHAT I ATE
- ☐ OTHER: _____

THIS RECHARGED ME THE MOST TODAY:

_____

_____

THOUGHTS I NEED TO CLEAR TO RELAX:

_____

_____

CHANGES I WANT TO MAKE FOR TOMORROW:

_____

_____

RECORD

DATE ____/____/____

GOALS FOR TODAY:

☐ _____
☐ _____
☐ _____

TO-DOS THAT CAN WAIT:

☐ _____
☐ _____
☐ _____

I'M EXCITED ABOUT:

_____
_____
_____

I'M STRESSED ABOUT:

_____
_____
_____

HOW I SPENT MY TIME (HOURS/MINUTES):

SLEEPING: _____

ON A SCREEN: _____

EXERCISING: _____

PLAYING: _____

BEING CREATIVE: _____

RELAXING: _____

WORKING: _____

EATING: _____

FOR MYSELF: _____

WITH FAMILY: _____

SOCIALIZING: _____

OTHER: _____

FOOD/DRINK I CONSUMED TODAY:

BREAKFAST

_____
_____
_____

LUNCH

_____
_____
_____

DINNER

_____
_____
_____

WATER/CAFFEINE (GLASSES/CUPS): 1   2   3   4   5   6   7   8

REFLECT

RATE YOUR ENERGY LEVEL TODAY:

1   2   3   4   5   6   7   8   9   10

MY ENERGY LEVEL WAS HIGHEST IN THE:
MORNING   AFTERNOON   EVENING

WHAT RECHARGED ME TODAY:

☐ TAKING A BATH   ☐ JOURNALING   ☐ BEING CREATIVE
☐ TAKING A NAP   ☐ SEEING A FRIEND   ☐ UNPLUGGING
☐ WALKING   ☐ TIME ALONE   ☐ TIME WITH FAMILY
☐ WORKING OUT   ☐ LISTENING TO   ☐ WHAT I ATE
☐ STRETCHING   MUSIC   ☐ OTHER:_____

THIS RECHARGED ME THE MOST TODAY:
_____
_____
_____

THOUGHTS I NEED TO CLEAR TO RELAX:
_____
_____
_____

CHANGES I WANT TO MAKE FOR TOMORROW:
_____
_____
_____

RECORD

DATE ___ / ___ / ___

GOALS FOR TODAY:

☐ _____
☐ _____
☐ _____

TO-DOS THAT CAN WAIT:

☐ _____
☐ _____
☐ _____

I'M EXCITED ABOUT:

_____
_____
_____

I'M STRESSED ABOUT:

_____
_____
_____

HOW I SPENT MY TIME (HOURS/MINUTES):

SLEEPING: _____

ON A SCREEN: _____

EXERCISING: _____

PLAYING: _____

BEING CREATIVE: _____

RELAXING: _____

WORKING: _____

EATING: _____

FOR MYSELF: _____

WITH FAMILY: _____

SOCIALIZING: _____

OTHER: _____

FOOD/DRINK I CONSUMED TODAY:

BREAKFAST

_____
_____
_____

LUNCH

_____
_____
_____

DINNER

_____
_____
_____

WATER/CAFFEINE (GLASSES/CUPS):   1   2   3   4   5   6   7   8

REFLECT

RATE YOUR ENERGY LEVEL TODAY:

1   2   3   4   5   6   7   8   9   10

MY ENERGY LEVEL WAS HIGHEST IN THE:

MORNING   AFTERNOON   EVENING

WHAT RECHARGED ME TODAY:

- [ ] TAKING A BATH
- [ ] TAKING A NAP
- [ ] WALKING
- [ ] WORKING OUT
- [ ] STRETCHING

- [ ] JOURNALING
- [ ] SEEING A FRIEND
- [ ] TIME ALONE
- [ ] LISTENING TO MUSIC

- [ ] BEING CREATIVE
- [ ] UNPLUGGING
- [ ] TIME WITH FAMILY
- [ ] WHAT I ATE
- [ ] OTHER:_____

THIS RECHARGED ME THE MOST TODAY:

_____

_____

_____

THOUGHTS I NEED TO CLEAR TO RELAX:

_____

_____

_____

CHANGES I WANT TO MAKE FOR TOMORROW:

_____

_____

_____

RECORD

DATE ___/___/___

GOALS FOR TODAY:

- ☐ ——————————————
- ☐ ——————————————
- ☐ ——————————————

TO-DOS THAT CAN WAIT:

- ☐ ——————————————
- ☐ ——————————————
- ☐ ——————————————

I'M EXCITED ABOUT:

——————————————
——————————————
——————————————

I'M STRESSED ABOUT:

——————————————
——————————————
——————————————

HOW I SPENT MY TIME (HOURS/MINUTES):

SLEEPING: _____

ON A SCREEN: _____

EXERCISING: _____

PLAYING: _____

BEING CREATIVE: _____

RELAXING: _____

WORKING: _____

EATING: _____

FOR MYSELF: _____

WITH FAMILY: _____

SOCIALIZING: _____

OTHER: _____

FOOD/DRINK I CONSUMED TODAY:

BREAKFAST

——————————————
——————————————
——————————————

LUNCH

——————————————
——————————————
——————————————

DINNER

——————————————
——————————————
——————————————

WATER/CAFFEINE (GLASSES/CUPS): 1   2   3   4   5   6   7   8

REFLECT

RATE YOUR ENERGY LEVEL TODAY:

1   2   3   4   5   6   7   8   9   10

MY ENERGY LEVEL WAS HIGHEST IN THE:

MORNING   AFTERNOON   EVENING

WHAT RECHARGED ME TODAY:

☐ TAKING A BATH   ☐ JOURNALING   ☐ BEING CREATIVE
☐ TAKING A NAP   ☐ SEEING A FRIEND   ☐ UNPLUGGING
☐ WALKING   ☐ TIME ALONE   ☐ TIME WITH FAMILY
☐ WORKING OUT   ☐ LISTENING TO   ☐ WHAT I ATE
☐ STRETCHING   MUSIC   ☐ OTHER:_____

THIS RECHARGED ME THE MOST TODAY:

_____
_____
_____

THOUGHTS I NEED TO CLEAR TO RELAX:

_____
_____
_____

CHANGES I WANT TO MAKE FOR TOMORROW:

_____
_____
_____

RECORD

DATE ___ / ___ / ___

GOALS FOR TODAY:

☐ _____
☐ _____
☐ _____

TO-DOS THAT CAN WAIT:

☐ _____
☐ _____
☐ _____

I'M EXCITED ABOUT:

_____
_____
_____

I'M STRESSED ABOUT:

_____
_____
_____

HOW I SPENT MY TIME (HOURS/MINUTES):

SLEEPING: _____

ON A SCREEN: _____

EXERCISING: _____

PLAYING: _____

BEING CREATIVE: _____

RELAXING: _____

WORKING: _____

EATING: _____

FOR MYSELF: _____

WITH FAMILY: _____

SOCIALIZING: _____

OTHER: _____

FOOD/DRINK I CONSUMED TODAY:

BREAKFAST

_____
_____
_____

LUNCH

_____
_____
_____

DINNER

_____
_____
_____

WATER/CAFFEINE (GLASSES/CUPS): 1 2 3 4 5 6 7 8

REFLECT

RATE YOUR ENERGY LEVEL TODAY:

1   2   3   4   5   6   7   8   9   10

MY ENERGY LEVEL WAS HIGHEST IN THE:

MORNING   AFTERNOON   EVENING

WHAT RECHARGED ME TODAY:

☐ TAKING A BATH   ☐ JOURNALING   ☐ BEING CREATIVE
☐ TAKING A NAP   ☐ SEEING A FRIEND ☐ UNPLUGGING
☐ WALKING   ☐ TIME ALONE   ☐ TIME WITH FAMILY
☐ WORKING OUT   ☐ LISTENING TO   ☐ WHAT I ATE
☐ STRETCHING   MUSIC   ☐ OTHER:_____

THIS RECHARGED ME THE MOST TODAY:

_____

_____

_____

THOUGHTS I NEED TO CLEAR TO RELAX:

_____

_____

_____

CHANGES I WANT TO MAKE FOR TOMORROW:

_____

_____

_____

RECORD

GOALS FOR TODAY:

☐ ————————————————
☐ ————————————————
☐ ————————————————

TO-DOS THAT CAN WAIT:

☐ ————————————————
☐ ————————————————
☐ ————————————————

I'M EXCITED ABOUT:

————————————————
————————————————
————————————————

I'M STRESSED ABOUT:

————————————————
————————————————
————————————————

HOW I SPENT MY TIME (HOURS/MINUTES):

SLEEPING: _____
ON A SCREEN: _____
EXERCISING: _____
PLAYING: _____
BEING CREATIVE: _____
RELAXING: _____

WORKING: _____
EATING: _____
FOR MYSELF: _____
WITH FAMILY: _____
SOCIALIZING: _____
OTHER: _____

FOOD/DRINK I CONSUMED TODAY:

BREAKFAST

————————————
————————————
————————————

LUNCH

————————————
————————————
————————————

DINNER

————————————
————————————
————————————

WATER/CAFFEINE (GLASSES/CUPS): 1   2   3   4   5   6   7   8

REFLECT

RATE YOUR ENERGY LEVEL TODAY:

1   2   3   4   5   6   7   8   9   10

MY ENERGY LEVEL WAS HIGHEST IN THE:

MORNING   AFTERNOON   EVENING

WHAT RECHARGED ME TODAY:

- [ ] TAKING A BATH
- [ ] TAKING A NAP
- [ ] WALKING
- [ ] WORKING OUT
- [ ] STRETCHING

- [ ] JOURNALING
- [ ] SEEING A FRIEND
- [ ] TIME ALONE
- [ ] LISTENING TO
     MUSIC

- [ ] BEING CREATIVE
- [ ] UNPLUGGING
- [ ] TIME WITH FAMILY
- [ ] WHAT I ATE
- [ ] OTHER:_____

THIS RECHARGED ME THE MOST TODAY:
_____
_____
_____

THOUGHTS I NEED TO CLEAR TO RELAX:
_____
_____
_____

CHANGES I WANT TO MAKE FOR TOMORROW:
_____
_____
_____

RECORD

DATE ___/___/___

GOALS FOR TODAY:

☐ ——————————————
☐ ——————————————
☐ ——————————————

TO-DOS THAT CAN WAIT:

☐ ——————————————
☐ ——————————————
☐ ——————————————

I'M EXCITED ABOUT:

——————————————
——————————————
——————————————

I'M STRESSED ABOUT:

——————————————
——————————————
——————————————

HOW I SPENT MY TIME (HOURS/MINUTES):

SLEEPING: _____

ON A SCREEN: _____

EXERCISING: _____

PLAYING: _____

BEING CREATIVE: _____

RELAXING: _____

WORKING: _____

EATING: _____

FOR MYSELF: _____

WITH FAMILY: _____

SOCIALIZING: _____

OTHER: _____

FOOD/DRINK I CONSUMED TODAY:

BREAKFAST

——————————————
——————————————
——————————————

LUNCH

——————————————
——————————————
——————————————

DINNER

——————————————
——————————————
——————————————

WATER/CAFFEINE (GLASSES/CUPS): 1   2   3   4   5   6   7   8

REFLECT

RATE YOUR ENERGY LEVEL TODAY:

1   2   3   4   5   6   7   8   9   10

MY ENERGY LEVEL WAS HIGHEST IN THE:

MORNING   AFTERNOON   EVENING

WHAT RECHARGED ME TODAY:

- [ ] TAKING A BATH
- [ ] TAKING A NAP
- [ ] WALKING
- [ ] WORKING OUT
- [ ] STRETCHING

- [ ] JOURNALING
- [ ] SEEING A FRIEND
- [ ] TIME ALONE
- [ ] LISTENING TO
      MUSIC

- [ ] BEING CREATIVE
- [ ] UNPLUGGING
- [ ] TIME WITH FAMILY
- [ ] WHAT I ATE
- [ ] OTHER:_____

THIS RECHARGED ME THE MOST TODAY:

_____
_____
_____

THOUGHTS I NEED TO CLEAR TO RELAX:

_____
_____
_____

CHANGES I WANT TO MAKE FOR TOMORROW:

_____
_____
_____

RECORD

DATE ___ / ___ / ___

GOALS FOR TODAY:

- ☐ _____
- ☐ _____
- ☐ _____

TO-DOS THAT CAN WAIT:

- ☐ _____
- ☐ _____
- ☐ _____

I'M EXCITED ABOUT:

_____
_____
_____

I'M STRESSED ABOUT:

_____
_____
_____

HOW I SPENT MY TIME (HOURS/MINUTES):

SLEEPING: _____

ON A SCREEN: _____

EXERCISING: _____

PLAYING: _____

BEING CREATIVE: _____

RELAXING: _____

WORKING: _____

EATING: _____

FOR MYSELF: _____

WITH FAMILY: _____

SOCIALIZING: _____

OTHER: _____

FOOD/DRINK I CONSUMED TODAY:

BREAKFAST

_____
_____
_____

LUNCH

_____
_____
_____

DINNER

_____
_____
_____

WATER/CAFFEINE (GLASSES/CUPS): 1 2 3 4 5 6 7 8

REFLECT

RATE YOUR ENERGY LEVEL TODAY:

1   2   3   4   5   6   7   8   9   10

MY ENERGY LEVEL WAS HIGHEST IN THE:

MORNING   AFTERNOON   EVENING

WHAT RECHARGED ME TODAY:

- [ ] TAKING A BATH
- [ ] TAKING A NAP
- [ ] WALKING
- [ ] WORKING OUT
- [ ] STRETCHING

- [ ] JOURNALING
- [ ] SEEING A FRIEND
- [ ] TIME ALONE
- [ ] LISTENING TO
      MUSIC

- [ ] BEING CREATIVE
- [ ] UNPLUGGING
- [ ] TIME WITH FAMILY
- [ ] WHAT I ATE
- [ ] OTHER:_____

THIS RECHARGED ME THE MOST TODAY:

_____
_____
_____

THOUGHTS I NEED TO CLEAR TO RELAX:

_____
_____
_____

CHANGES I WANT TO MAKE FOR TOMORROW:

_____
_____
_____

RECORD

DATE ___ / ___ / ___

GOALS FOR TODAY:

- [ ] _____
- [ ] _____
- [ ] _____

TO-DOS THAT CAN WAIT:

- [ ] _____
- [ ] _____
- [ ] _____

I'M EXCITED ABOUT:

_____
_____
_____

I'M STRESSED ABOUT:

_____
_____
_____

HOW I SPENT MY TIME (HOURS/MINUTES):

SLEEPING: _____   WORKING: _____

ON A SCREEN: _____   EATING: _____

EXERCISING: _____   FOR MYSELF: _____

PLAYING: _____   WITH FAMILY: _____

BEING CREATIVE: _____   SOCIALIZING: _____

RELAXING: _____   OTHER: _____

FOOD/DRINK I CONSUMED TODAY:

BREAKFAST   LUNCH   DINNER

_____   _____   _____
_____   _____   _____
_____   _____   _____

WATER/CAFFEINE (GLASSES/CUPS):   1   2   3   4   5   6   7   8

REFLECT

RATE YOUR ENERGY LEVEL TODAY:

1   2   3   4   5   6   7   8   9   10

MY ENERGY LEVEL WAS HIGHEST IN THE:

MORNING   AFTERNOON   EVENING

WHAT RECHARGED ME TODAY:

☐ TAKING A BATH   ☐ JOURNALING   ☐ BEING CREATIVE
☐ TAKING A NAP   ☐ SEEING A FRIEND   ☐ UNPLUGGING
☐ WALKING   ☐ TIME ALONE   ☐ TIME WITH FAMILY
☐ WORKING OUT   ☐ LISTENING TO   ☐ WHAT I ATE
☐ STRETCHING   MUSIC   ☐ OTHER:_____

THIS RECHARGED ME THE MOST TODAY:

_____
_____
_____

THOUGHTS I NEED TO CLEAR TO RELAX:

_____
_____
_____

CHANGES I WANT TO MAKE FOR TOMORROW:

_____
_____
_____

RECORD

DATE ___ / ___ / ___

GOALS FOR TODAY:

☐ _____
☐ _____
☐ _____

TO-DOS THAT CAN WAIT:

☐ _____
☐ _____
☐ _____

I'M EXCITED ABOUT:

_____
_____
_____

I'M STRESSED ABOUT:

_____
_____
_____

HOW I SPENT MY TIME (HOURS/MINUTES):

SLEEPING: _____

ON A SCREEN: _____

EXERCISING: _____

PLAYING: _____

BEING CREATIVE: _____

RELAXING: _____

WORKING: _____

EATING: _____

FOR MYSELF: _____

WITH FAMILY: _____

SOCIALIZING: _____

OTHER: _____

FOOD/DRINK I CONSUMED TODAY:

BREAKFAST

_____
_____
_____

LUNCH

_____
_____
_____

DINNER

_____
_____
_____

WATER/CAFFEINE (GLASSES/CUPS): 1 2 3 4 5 6 7 8

REFLECT

RATE YOUR ENERGY LEVEL TODAY:

1   2   3   4   5   6   7   8   9   10

MY ENERGY LEVEL WAS HIGHEST IN THE:

MORNING   AFTERNOON   EVENING

WHAT RECHARGED ME TODAY:

- ☐ TAKING A BATH
- ☐ TAKING A NAP
- ☐ WALKING
- ☐ WORKING OUT
- ☐ STRETCHING

- ☐ JOURNALING
- ☐ SEEING A FRIEND
- ☐ TIME ALONE
- ☐ LISTENING TO
  MUSIC

- ☐ BEING CREATIVE
- ☐ UNPLUGGING
- ☐ TIME WITH FAMILY
- ☐ WHAT I ATE
- ☐ OTHER:_____

THIS RECHARGED ME THE MOST TODAY:

_____

_____

_____

THOUGHTS I NEED TO CLEAR TO RELAX:

_____

_____

_____

CHANGES I WANT TO MAKE FOR TOMORROW:

_____

_____

_____

RECORD

DATE ___/___/___

GOALS FOR TODAY:

☐ ————————————————
☐ ————————————————
☐ ————————————————

TO-DOS THAT CAN WAIT:

☐ ————————————————
☐ ————————————————
☐ ————————————————

I'M EXCITED ABOUT:

————————————————————
————————————————————
————————————————————

I'M STRESSED ABOUT:

————————————————————
————————————————————
————————————————————

HOW I SPENT MY TIME (HOURS/MINUTES):

SLEEPING: _____

ON A SCREEN: _____

EXERCISING: _____

PLAYING: _____

BEING CREATIVE: _____

RELAXING: _____

WORKING: _____

EATING: _____

FOR MYSELF: _____

WITH FAMILY: _____

SOCIALIZING: _____

OTHER: _____

FOOD/DRINK I CONSUMED TODAY:

BREAKFAST

————————————
————————————
————————————

LUNCH

————————————
————————————
————————————

DINNER

————————————
————————————
————————————

WATER/CAFFEINE (GLASSES/CUPS): 1   2   3   4   5   6   7   8

REFLECT

RATE YOUR ENERGY LEVEL TODAY:

1   2   3   4   5   6   7   8   9   10

MY ENERGY LEVEL WAS HIGHEST IN THE:
MORNING   AFTERNOON   EVENING

WHAT RECHARGED ME TODAY:

☐ TAKING A BATH   ☐ JOURNALING   ☐ BEING CREATIVE
☐ TAKING A NAP   ☐ SEEING A FRIEND   ☐ UNPLUGGING
☐ WALKING   ☐ TIME ALONE   ☐ TIME WITH FAMILY
☐ WORKING OUT   ☐ LISTENING TO   ☐ WHAT I ATE
☐ STRETCHING   MUSIC   ☐ OTHER: _____

THIS RECHARGED ME THE MOST TODAY:
_____
_____
_____

THOUGHTS I NEED TO CLEAR TO RELAX:
_____
_____
_____

CHANGES I WANT TO MAKE FOR TOMORROW:
_____
_____
_____

RECORD

DATE ___/___/___

GOALS FOR TODAY:

☐ _____
☐ _____
☐ _____

TO-DOS THAT CAN WAIT:

☐ _____
☐ _____
☐ _____

I'M EXCITED ABOUT:

_____
_____
_____

I'M STRESSED ABOUT:

_____
_____
_____

HOW I SPENT MY TIME (HOURS/MINUTES):

SLEEPING: _____   WORKING: _____

ON A SCREEN: _____   EATING: _____

EXERCISING: _____   FOR MYSELF: _____

PLAYING: _____   WITH FAMILY: _____

BEING CREATIVE: _____   SOCIALIZING: _____

RELAXING: _____   OTHER: _____

FOOD/DRINK I CONSUMED TODAY:

BREAKFAST   LUNCH   DINNER

_____   _____   _____
_____   _____   _____

WATER/CAFFEINE (GLASSES/CUPS): 1   2   3   4   5   6   7   8

REFLECT

RATE YOUR ENERGY LEVEL TODAY:

1   2   3   4   5   6   7   8   9   10

MY ENERGY LEVEL WAS HIGHEST IN THE:

MORNING   AFTERNOON   EVENING

WHAT RECHARGED ME TODAY:

☐ TAKING A BATH   ☐ JOURNALING   ☐ BEING CREATIVE
☐ TAKING A NAP   ☐ SEEING A FRIEND   ☐ UNPLUGGING
☐ WALKING   ☐ TIME ALONE   ☐ TIME WITH FAMILY
☐ WORKING OUT   ☐ LISTENING TO   ☐ WHAT I ATE
☐ STRETCHING   MUSIC   ☐ OTHER:_____

THIS RECHARGED ME THE MOST TODAY:
_____
_____
_____

THOUGHTS I NEED TO CLEAR TO RELAX:
_____
_____
_____

CHANGES I WANT TO MAKE FOR TOMORROW:
_____
_____
_____

RECORD

DATE ___ / ___ / ___

GOALS FOR TODAY:

☐ _____
☐ _____
☐ _____

TO-DOS THAT CAN WAIT:

☐ _____
☐ _____
☐ _____

I'M EXCITED ABOUT:

_____
_____
_____

I'M STRESSED ABOUT:

_____
_____
_____

HOW I SPENT MY TIME (HOURS/MINUTES):

SLEEPING: _____ WORKING: _____

ON A SCREEN: _____ EATING: _____

EXERCISING: _____ FOR MYSELF: _____

PLAYING: _____ WITH FAMILY: _____

BEING CREATIVE: _____ SOCIALIZING: _____

RELAXING: _____ OTHER: _____

FOOD/DRINK I CONSUMED TODAY:

BREAKFAST   LUNCH   DINNER

_____   _____   _____
_____   _____   _____
_____   _____   _____

WATER/CAFFEINE (GLASSES/CUPS):   1   2   3   4   5   6   7   8

REFLECT

RATE YOUR ENERGY LEVEL TODAY:

1   2   3   4   5   6   7   8   9   10

MY ENERGY LEVEL WAS HIGHEST IN THE:

MORNING   AFTERNOON   EVENING

WHAT RECHARGED ME TODAY:

☐ TAKING A BATH   ☐ JOURNALING   ☐ BEING CREATIVE
☐ TAKING A NAP   ☐ SEEING A FRIEND   ☐ UNPLUGGING
☐ WALKING   ☐ TIME ALONE   ☐ TIME WITH FAMILY
☐ WORKING OUT   ☐ LISTENING TO   ☐ WHAT I ATE
☐ STRETCHING   MUSIC   ☐ OTHER:_____

THIS RECHARGED ME THE MOST TODAY:

_____
_____
_____

THOUGHTS I NEED TO CLEAR TO RELAX:

_____
_____
_____

CHANGES I WANT TO MAKE FOR TOMORROW:

_____
_____
_____

RECORD

DATE ___/___/___

GOALS FOR TODAY:

- ☐ ————————————————
- ☐ ————————————————
- ☐ ————————————————

TO-DOS THAT CAN WAIT:

- ☐ ————————————————
- ☐ ————————————————
- ☐ ————————————————

I'M EXCITED ABOUT:

————————————————
————————————————
————————————————

I'M STRESSED ABOUT:

————————————————
————————————————
————————————————

HOW I SPENT MY TIME (HOURS/MINUTES):

SLEEPING: _____

ON A SCREEN: _____

EXERCISING: _____

PLAYING: _____

BEING CREATIVE: _____

RELAXING: _____

WORKING: _____

EATING: _____

FOR MYSELF: _____

WITH FAMILY: _____

SOCIALIZING: _____

OTHER: _____

FOOD/DRINK I CONSUMED TODAY:

BREAKFAST

————————————————
————————————————
————————————————

LUNCH

————————————————
————————————————
————————————————

DINNER

————————————————
————————————————
————————————————

WATER/CAFFEINE (GLASSES/CUPS): 1   2   3   4   5   6   7   8

REFLECT

RATE YOUR ENERGY LEVEL TODAY:

1   2   3   4   5   6   7   8   9   10

MY ENERGY LEVEL WAS HIGHEST IN THE:

MORNING   AFTERNOON   EVENING

WHAT RECHARGED ME TODAY:

- ☐ TAKING A BATH
- ☐ TAKING A NAP
- ☐ WALKING
- ☐ WORKING OUT
- ☐ STRETCHING

- ☐ JOURNALING
- ☐ SEEING A FRIEND
- ☐ TIME ALONE
- ☐ LISTENING TO
   MUSIC

- ☐ BEING CREATIVE
- ☐ UNPLUGGING
- ☐ TIME WITH FAMILY
- ☐ WHAT I ATE
- ☐ OTHER:_____

THIS RECHARGED ME THE MOST TODAY:

_____
_____
_____

THOUGHTS I NEED TO CLEAR TO RELAX:

_____
_____
_____

CHANGES I WANT TO MAKE FOR TOMORROW:

_____
_____
_____

RECORD

DATE ___/___/___

GOALS FOR TODAY:

☐ ——————————————
☐ ——————————————
☐ ——————————————

TO-DOS THAT CAN WAIT:

☐ ——————————————
☐ ——————————————
☐ ——————————————

I'M EXCITED ABOUT:

——————————————
——————————————
——————————————

I'M STRESSED ABOUT:

——————————————
——————————————
——————————————

HOW I SPENT MY TIME (HOURS/MINUTES):

SLEEPING: _____

ON A SCREEN: _____

EXERCISING: _____

PLAYING: _____

BEING CREATIVE: _____

RELAXING: _____

WORKING: _____

EATING: _____

FOR MYSELF: _____

WITH FAMILY: _____

SOCIALIZING: _____

OTHER: _____

FOOD/DRINK I CONSUMED TODAY:

BREAKFAST

——————————
——————————
——————————

LUNCH

——————————
——————————
——————————

DINNER

——————————
——————————
——————————

WATER/CAFFEINE (GLASSES/CUPS):   1   2   3   4   5   6   7   8

REFLECT

RATE YOUR ENERGY LEVEL TODAY:

1   2   3   4   5   6   7   8   9   10

MY ENERGY LEVEL WAS HIGHEST IN THE:

MORNING   AFTERNOON   EVENING

WHAT RECHARGED ME TODAY:

- [ ] TAKING A BATH
- [ ] TAKING A NAP
- [ ] WALKING
- [ ] WORKING OUT
- [ ] STRETCHING

- [ ] JOURNALING
- [ ] SEEING A FRIEND
- [ ] TIME ALONE
- [ ] LISTENING TO MUSIC

- [ ] BEING CREATIVE
- [ ] UNPLUGGING
- [ ] TIME WITH FAMILY
- [ ] WHAT I ATE
- [ ] OTHER:_____

THIS RECHARGED ME THE MOST TODAY:
_____
_____
_____

THOUGHTS I NEED TO CLEAR TO RELAX:
_____
_____
_____

CHANGES I WANT TO MAKE FOR TOMORROW:
_____
_____
_____